Twayne's English Authors Series

Sylvia E. Bowman, *Editor*

INDIANA UNIVERSITY

Matthew Arnold

MATTHEW ARNOLD

Matthew Arnold

By FRASER NEIMAN

College of William and Mary

Twayne Publishers, Inc.   ::   New York

FOR
F. D.
C. F.
T. & P.

MATTHEW ARNOLD

by

FRASER NEIMAN

Matthew Arnold has compelled the interest of readers for over a century. He began his literary career in 1849 with a book of poems expressing for his generation a sense of the isolation of the individual and of confinement in a time of bewildering and rapid intellectual change. He addressed himself to large topics of educational reform in his writings, and to the contests between science and orthodoxy, between the utilitarian and humanistic spirit, and between English political stubbornness and Irish rancor. His controlling objective was the civilizing of the individual, and in an age of diminishing religious commitment he urged the use of literature as a main agent in man's humanization. The integrity of Arnold's poetry and the sanity of his literary criticism have insured him continuing esteem, while much of his poetry and criticism remains directly relevant to our own time.

The present book is addressed to the general reader and to students and teachers who wish to know something of his careers, the range of his intellectual interests, and the character of his poetry and criticism. Dr. Neiman presents Arnold as a coherent figure, a man whose wide-ranging interests are controlled by the conviction that reason and patient individual endeavor will always

create civilization out of any conditions of change. Like William Faulkner, he was persuaded that man can prevail.

Preface

Matthew Arnold desired not to have an official biography written of him, and scholars have respected this request. The advantage has been the number of thoughtful critical examinations that have been made of particular aspects of his many-sided career as poet, educator, and critic of society and literature. In this short book I wish to introduce to the student and the general reader Arnold's diverse activities and his main intellectual interests. Biographical data is, I hope, subordinated to interpretive comment on his writings.

Arnold gives the modern reader a way of seeing the mid-Victorian period; he also speaks directly to us at many points, for he was continuously concerned with humanistic ideals. Early in his life he admired the novels of George Sand because she expressed aspiration towards a purged and renewed human society. This aspiration gives centrality and continuity to his own activities. For, despite his diversity of activity, Arnold is an integrated personality. I interpret Arnold in this book as I understand him; I do not attempt to make a digest of Arnoldian criticism. The selected bibliography that I have provided partially expresses the debt that I inevitably owe to the numerous scholars who have contributed to a fuller understanding of Arnold's work. I hope it will lead the inquiring reader to a variety of informative and provocative discussions.

Besides the obligation I owe to many students of Arnold, both those unnamed and those named in the notes and the brief bibliography of this book, I wish to thank Professor William B. Guthrie of the University of Richmond for allowing me to consult his copy of his dissertation on the unpublished portions of Arnold's diaries, the library staffs of the College of William and Mary, Bowdoin College, and Harvard University for many services. I also thank the College of William and Mary for grants-in-aid that made possible some leisure for the preparation of the book.

A considerable part of Chapter VII is revised from my article "The Zeitgeist of Matthew Arnold" and is used by permission of the Modern Language Association from *PMLA*, LXXII (1957), 977-96. The Oxford University Press has kindly given me permission to make frequent quotations from H. F. Lowry, *The Letters of Matthew Arnold to Arthur Hugh Clough.*

I also wish to thank Mrs. Eleanor P. Abbot for helpful suggestions about my manuscript, Miss Susan Szadowkierski and Mrs. Linda N. Schilling for their aid in preparing it for publication, and my wife for making the index. Professor Sylvia Bowman's editorial aid has been very generous and very valuable.

The College of William and Mary   Fraser Neiman
Williamsburg, Virginia

Contents

Preface

Chronology

1. Laleham, Rugby, Oxford   13

2. "The Tragic Imperatives"   30

3. The Inspector of Schools   46

4. The Defense of Poetry   58

5. "The Hideous Title of 'Professor'"   81

6. Anarchy and Authority   100

7. *Geist* and the *Zeitgeist*   113

8. "Skies of Brass and Iron"   136

9. "A Far-Set Goal"   150

Notes and References   165

Selected Bibliography   179

Index   185

Chronology

1822   Matthew Arnold born December 24 at Laleham-on-Thames, Surrey, England.

1828   Moved to Rugby when his father, Dr. Thomas Arnold, became Headmaster.

1836-
1840   Student at Winchester School (summer, 1836, to autumn, 1837). Visited northern France, August, 1836, with his parents. Student at Rugby, September, 1837, to June, 1840. Won Rugby Poetry Prize for *Alaric at Rome*. Won scholarship to Balliol College, Oxford.

1841   Entered Balliol College, October 15. Dr. Arnold appointed Regius Professor of Modern History at Oxford.

1842   Tied for second place for Hertford Latin Scholarship at Oxford in March. Dr. Arnold died suddenly, on June 12, at the age of forty-seven.

1843   Won Newdigate Poetry Prize with *Cromwell*.

1844   Took his bachelor's degree with second-class honors in *Litterae Humaniores*.

1845   Taught Classics at Rugby as temporary assistant-master in February and March. Elected to Fellowship at Oriel College, Oxford, in March.

1846   Traveled in France and Switzerland; visited Paris from December, 1846, to February, 1847.

1847   Became private secretary to Henry Petty-Fitzmaurice, third Marquis of Lansdowne.

1849   *The Strayed Reveller, and Other Poems,* "by A," published in February.

1850   "Memorial Verses" published in *Fraser's Magazine* in June.

1851   Appointed in April to an Inspectorship of Schools. Married in June at Teddington to Frances Lucy, daughter of Sir William Wightman, a judge of the Court of the Queen's Bench.

1852   *Empedocles on Etna, and Other Poems* by "A."

1853   *Poems: A New Edition,* published under his own name.

1855   *Poems, Second Series.*

1856   First American edition of *Poems. A New and Complete Edition.*

1857   Elected in May to chair of Professor of Poetry at Oxford. His inaugural lecture "On the Modern Element in Literature," delivered in the Sheldonian Theatre in November. *Merope* published in December with title page dated 1858.

1858   Began settled residence in London at 2 Chester Square.

1859   Appointed foreign assistant commissioner of the Duke of Newcastle's Commission to study elementary education in England. Met Sainte-Beuve in Paris in August. *England and the Italian Question* published. Elected member of Alpine Club, London. Served in the autumn in the Queen's Westminster Rifle Volunteers.

1860   *Report to the Education Commission—Confidential Edition.*

1861   Delivered the Oxford Lectures, "On Translating Homer." *The Popular Education of France; with notices of that of Holland and Switzerland,* the public edition of his Education Commission report. Arthur Hugh Clough died in Florence, November 13. *On Translating Homer: Three Lectures given at Oxford.*

1862   Re-elected for another five years to the Poetry Chair at Oxford. In March, "The Twice-Revised Code" in *Fraser's Magazine. On Translating Homer: Last Words.*

1864   *A French Eton; or, Middle Class Education and the State.* "The Literary Influence of Academies" in the *Cornhill Magazine* and "The Function of Criticism at the Present Time" in the *National Review* established Arnold's characteristic role as what Henry James called a *general* critic.

1865   *Essays in Criticism,* (designated after 1888 as *Essays in Criticism, First Series*). Appointed assistant commissioner on the Schools Inquiry Commission to report on secondary schools and universities in France, Germany, Switzerland, and Italy.

1866   In April, "Thyrsis" in *Macmillan's Magazine.* Applied unsuccessfully for a Charity Commissionership as an alternative to his Inspectorship.

1867   *New Poems* and *On the Study of Celtic Literature,* which comprised the lectures delivered at Oxford in 1866. Sought unsuccessfully the librarianship of the House of Commons.

1868   Moved to Byron House, Harrow, in April. Infant son Basil died in January; eldest son Thomas, an invalid, died aged sixteen in November. *Schools and Universities on the Continent.*

1869   *Culture and Anarchy. Poems,* first collected edition. Sought commissionership under the Endowed Schools Act, but appointment was successfully opposed by Gladstone.

1870   *St. Paul and Protestantism.* Promoted to senior inspectorship of schools. Awarded honorary degree of D.C.L. by the University of Oxford.

1871   *Friendship's Garland.*

1872   Son William Trevenen died, aged eighteen. Edited *A Bible-Reading for Schools; The Great Prophecy of Israel's Restoration.*

1873   *Literature and Dogma.* Moved to Pains Hill Cottage, Cobham, Surrey.

1874   *Higher Schools and Universities in Germany.*

1875   *God and the Bible: A Review of Objections to "Literature and Dogma";* edited *Isaiah XL-LXVI, with the Shorter Prophecies Allied to It.*

1876   *La Crise religieuse,* a translation by Dr. Charles Sarazin of *Literature and Dogma* published in Paris.

1877   *Last Essays on Church and Religion* and *Poems,* the second collected edition. Declined to stand for election as Lord Rector of St. Andrews University.

1878   *Selected Poems of Matthew Arnold.* Edited *The Six Chief Lives from Johnson's "Lives of the Poets."*

1879   *Mixed Essays.* Edited with a critical preface *Poems* of Wordsworth.

1880   Wrote a general introduction and essays on Thomas Gray and John Keats for T.H. Ward's *The English Poets.*

1881   *Poems,* a re-issue of the 1877 edition. Edited a selection of *Letters, Speeches and Tracts on Irish Affairs by Edmund Burke.* Edited with a prefatory critical essay *Poetry of Byron.*

1882   *Irish Essays and Others.* Delivered the Rede Lecture at

Cambridge University on "Literature and Science" in May. Delivered at University College, Liverpool, "A Liverpool Address."

1883 Awarded by Gladstone a Civil List pension "as a public recognition of service to the poetry and literature of England." October, 1883, to March, 1884, lectured in America. Edited *Isaiah of Jerusalem in the Authorized English Version with an Introduction, Corrections, and Notes.*

1884 Promoted to a chief inspectorship of schools.

1885 The American lectures published as *Discourses in America.* Published *Poems*, in three volumes.

1886 Second trip to America. Contributed "Charles Augustin Sainte-Beuve" to *Encyclopaedia Britannica* (Ninth Edition). Resigned inspectorship of schools in April.

1887 Contributed "Schools" to *The Reign of Queen Victoria,* ed. T. H. Ward.

1888 Died suddenly of a heart attack in Liverpool on April 15. *Essays in Criticism, Second Series,* published posthumously. *Civilization in the United States: First and Last Impressions of America* published in Boston.

1889 *Reports on Elementary Schools, 1852-1882,* ed. by Sir Francis Sandford.

CHAPTER 1

Laleham, Rugby, Oxford

WHEN Matthew Arnold first visited America and compared reality with his preconceptions, young Henry James had already spent several years in England with the intention of penetrating the barriers of European, and especially of English, life. In the January issue of the *English Illustrated Magazine* in 1884, James declared that for the American, or indeed for any other visitor to England, Matthew Arnold speaks "more directly than any contemporary English writer, says more of these things which make him the visitor's intellectual companion."[1] Matthew Arnold is, James observed, "among the English writers of our own day, the least matter-of-fact Englishman. . . . And yet he is 'en fin de compte' (as the foreigner might say) English of the English."

Like Henry James, we are in a sense all strangers in Victorian England. If we seek to enter it, Arnold remains for us also—by virtue of his multiple interests and by the light in which he views them—a guide to an extraordinary number of facets of four troubled decades, from 1848 to 1888, the year of his death. The titles of a few modern studies of him—*The Educational Thought and Influence of Matthew Arnold* (1950), *The Ethical Idealism of Matthew Arnold* (1959), *Matthew Arnold and the Romantics* (1963), *Matthew Arnold and the Three Classes* (1964)—suggest in themselves something of the range of Victorian thought to which his writings can introduce the twentieth-century visitor. As a poet, he voices the dilemma of orthodox faith, the awareness of intellectual and social change, and the sense of individual isolation in the cosmos—all of which many Victorians shared. He confronted these issues with a humanistic Stoicism that strongly characterizes him.

Henry James discerned in Arnold not only a guide to intellectual interests, but a personality as well. The frequent indifference of the late Victorian Englishman to foreign modes of life, his serene complacency, his assumption that his way is the normal one—all constitute, James wrote, "a huge blank surface, a mighty national wall, against which the perceptive, the critical effort of the presumptuous stranger wastes itself, until after a little, he espies in the measureless spaces, a little aperture, a window which is suddenly thrown open, and at which a friendly intelligent face is presented, the harbinger of a voice of greeting."[2] By 1884, Arnold's voice of greeting had achieved, for some rhetorical purposes, its own tone of serene complacency; but Arnold had directed his effort to penetrating the national wall, opening it to intellectual attitudes of the Continent, disturbing the insularity of many popular ideas, notably those of "That wonderful creature, the British Philistine."[3]

Swinburne once quoted a witty critic who referred to Matthew Arnold as "David, the son of Goliath."[4] It is true that in many areas Arnold felt himself to be his father's continuator. And in no endeavor more than that of measuring English intellectual achievement by wide European standards did Arnold actively pursue the work of Dr. Thomas Arnold. However, to his father's cosmopolitan intellectual sympathies, he added his own poetic imaginativeness and his more critical esthetic sensibility. In 1869, when he finished reading a biography of his own godfather, the Reverend John Keble, Matthew Arnold wrote to his mother: "There is much to interest me, and there must be more to interest you; but my own feeling when I close the book is of papa's immense superiority to all the set, mainly because, owing to his historic sense, he was so wonderfully, for his nation, time, and profession, European, and thus so got himself out of the narrow medium in which, after all, his English friends lived."[5] It is in a large measure because of the complexity of the medium in which he lived that the son remains an expert guide.

During the fifteen years from 1830 to 1845—the years of Arnold's schooling—political events occurred and intellectual attitudes were shaped that continued in ever-modifying forms to dominate another two decades. We can only enumerate, by way of reminder, a few notable achievements of those years of turbulent change. In 1830, the accession of William IV brought an end to Wellington's Tory ministry and made possible the entry into office of a Whig ministry under Earl Grey. The revived interest in parliamentary reforms culminated, for the moment, in the passage two years later of the "Great" Reform Bill. Triumphant in itself, as Thomas Babington Macaulay thought it was, this bill only began the movement towards political democracy that continued through the century—to the deep misgivings of Thomas Carlyle and the increasing confidence of Matthew Arnold. In 1830, man's inevitable confrontation by geology and astronomy—the "Terrible Muses" Tennyson called them—and his attendant sense of his isolation in the universe were deepened by the publication of the first part of Sir Charles Lyell's *Principles of Geology.* The *Principles,* however cautiously worded, admitted the creation of man "at a comparatively modern epoch" and allowed the inference that change may work by blind processes.

Also in 1830 Henry Hart Milman, who like Dr. Richard Whately and Dr. Thomas Arnold was a leader in liberal Broad Church theology at Oxford, published in the *History of the Jews* a realistic interpretation of Old Testament history that treated Abraham as an Arab Sheik. Moreover, David Friedrich Strauss's *Life of Jesus* (1835), which George Eliot translated in 1846, popularized the skeptical tendency of German historical criticism of biblical texts. Between 1830 and 1835 not only did these and other expressions of religious liberalism, such as Dr. Arnold's *Principles of Church Reform* (1833) develop, but the religiously conservative Tractarian, or Oxford, movement also began. By ironic chance, a climax in the history of that movement was reached on October 9, 1845. On that day John Henry Newman, one of its great initiators, left the Church of England for the Roman Catholic Church, while Ernest Renan withdrew from the Seminary of St. Sulpice, a withdrawal that symbolized the force of secularist thought in the century. The work of the evangelical side of the Broad Church movement within the Church of England was concerned not only with liberal theology but also with good works; of these, the abolition of slavery throughout the dominions in 1833 was the triumph of William Wilberforce. The event was a symbol of that continuous humanitarian effort that is so marked an element of the Victorian social conscience.

In the world of letters the years of Matthew Arnold's boyhood appear to be a watershed. By 1832, when Goethe and Sir Walter Scott, two great exemplars of European Romanticism died, Samuel Taylor Coleridge, Charles Lamb, Thomas DeQuincey, and William Wordsworth alone remained of the major figures of English Romanticism, and only Wordsworth and DeQuincey survived into Victoria's reign. But on the other hand, by 1832 the new men—Macaulay, Alfred Tennyson, and Charles Dickens —had begun to publish; by the end of Matthew Arnold's undergraduate career at Oxford, W. M. Thackeray, Benjamin Disraeli, Robert Browning, George Eliot, John Stuart Mill, and John Ruskin were active.

I *Boyhood and Schooling*

In 1819 the Reverend Thomas Arnold settled at Laleham on the Thames with his widowed mother, Martha Delafield Arnold, his aunt Frances Arnold, and his youngest sister Susanna. A graduate of Oxford, a late Fellow of Oriel College, and an ordained deacon, Arnold and the Reverend John Buckland jointly ran a school at Laleham. Buckland was married to Dr. Arnold's sister Frances. In 1820 Arnold himself married Mary Penrose, daughter of John Penrose, the rector of Fledborough, and of Jane Trevenen Penrose. He settled into a strenuous career as master of the upper division of the Laleham school and as the supporter of an increasing family.

Their first child, born in 1821, was Jane Martha. She is the "Fausta" of Arnold's poem "Resignation," and the "K" of his correspondence; and she became the wife of the Liberal Member of Parliament and educator, W. E. Forster. Matthew was born on December 24, 1822. Among his younger sisters, Mary, Frances, and Susanna, the second, "Fan" (b. 1833), remained the companion of her mother and one of her brother's constant correspondents. Among his four brothers, Thomas (b. 1823) was the closest to Matthew in age, and for some years in interest. He was Matt's contemporary at Oxford, although he attended University College while his brother was at Balliol; and, like him, Thomas confronted the winds of Tractarian controversy. Unlike Matthew, Tom Arnold—waveringly, for he was twice converted

—followed John Henry Newman into the Roman Catholic Church. He emigrated to New Zealand in 1845, and he became the father of Mary Augusta Ward, the novelist, better known as Mrs. Humphry Ward. Of the other brothers, William Delafield Arnold (b. 1827) was the author of a novel, *Oakfield or Fellowship in the East.* He is the subject of two of Matthew's elegiac poems —"Stanzas at Carnac" and "A Southern Night."

In 1828, Dr. Arnold was appointed Headmaster of Rugby; and the Arnolds moved to a new home. But Matthew returned to school at Laleham in 1830 and remained there until the autumn of 1833. He regarded Laleham fondly, and in the tragic year 1868 he buried his own oldest and his youngest sons there, and a third in 1872. His fullest recollection of Laleham is recorded in a letter that he, then private secretary to Lord Lansdowne, the influential but aging Whig peer, wrote to his mother on January 2, 1848:

Last Monday I went to Laleham. . . . It was nearly dark when I left the Weybridge Station, but I could make out the wide sheet of the gray Thames gleaming through the general dusk as I came out on Chertsey Bridge. I never go along that shelving gravelly road up towards Laleham without interest, from Chertsey Lock to the turn where the drunken man lay. To-day, after morning church, I went up to Pentonhook, and found the stream with the old volume, width, shine, rapid fulness, "kempshott," and swans, unchanged and un-equalled, to my partial and remembering eyes at least. On the Hook itself they have been draining and cutting a little; but the old paved part of the barge road on the Laleham side of the Lock-house is all as it was, and the campanulas, they told me, grow as much as ever there in summer. Yesterday I was at Chertsey, the poetic town of our childhood as opposed to the practical, historical Staines: it is *across* the river, reached by no bridges and roads, but by the primitive ferry; the meadow path, the Abbey river with its wooden bridge and the narrow lane by the old wall; and, itself the stillest of the country towns backed by St. Ann's, leads nowhere but to the heaths and pines of Surrey. How unlike the journey to Staines, and the great road through the flat, drained Middlesex plain, with its single standing pollarded elms! I was yesterday at the old house and under the cedars and by the old pink acacia. I went to see Mrs. Powell and Mrs. Nokes, the first of whom, at eighty, recalls her charwoman days, and her puff paste which did not give satisfaction because Mr. Buckland preferred short paste—and thanks the dear Lord that she can still do for herself.

The second is in extreme feebleness, but she, too, remembered the Whitmonday on which that nice man, Mr. Arnold, when no one came from Staines, took the duty himself, etc, etc.[6]

The years of Arnold's later childhood were divided between the summer home at Fox How near Ambleside in the Lake District and the winter home at Rugby. Fox How, which Dr. Arnold built about 1834 or 1835, brought the Arnolds in close touch with the Wordsworth circle; it remained the home of Dr. Arnold's widow, and a center of Matthew Arnold's affectionate interest, until his mother's death in 1873.

In 1827, the Trustees of Rugby School began to seek a head-master to succeed Dr. John Wooll. Arthur Stanley described Rugby at that time as "a fair average specimen of the public schools."[7] It was typical in its rigid and narrowly classical curriculum, in its system of fagging and bullying, and in its intention to train an élite who, after Oxford or Cambridge careers, would take their places as "gentlemen" in positions of political or professional influence. The modern historian E. L. Woodward reminds us that, "When the duke of Wellington talked about the playing-fields of Eton, he had in mind not games but fighting."[8] In his testimonial supporting Dr. Arnold's candidacy, Dr. Edward Hawkins, later Provost of Oriel, predicted that, "if Mr. Arnold were elected to the head-mastership of Rugby, he would change the face of education all through the public schools of England."[9]

To the appointment that he entered upon in August, 1828, Thomas Arnold brought his great and cheerful energy, his piety and dedication, his Classical scholarship, and his educational and political liberalism. "He is one of those persons," John Keble said of him, "whom it does me good to think of when I am in a grumbling vein."[10] And Keble wrote in 1828 to John Taylor Coleridge, a nephew of Samuel Taylor Coleridge: "I heard yesterday from Arnold, who seems to be fast taking root at Rugby, and will soon fill the school I dare say. I only hope he will not teach them his own notions of right and wrong in politics. . . . I very much admire the sort of cheerful, straightforward way, in which Tommy sets out on his new career. I am sure he is right, and much to be imitated in that, whatever he may be in his notions about some matters."[11]

Dr. Arnold brought to Rugby the reforming spirit that Dr. Hawkins anticipated, and he expressed the social and political liberalism that Keble feared. He made French and mathematics central to the curriculum at Rugby; he added German; he taught classics not only for syntax but for content, as an introduction to social and political life; he raised the level of discipline and strove to set a high moral tone. His discourses in Rugby Chapel made it the focus of the school life. Religious and moral principles, gentlemanly conduct, intellectual ability in that order were the qualities he sought to develop in the Rugby student.[12]

A reformer in a reforming age, Dr. Arnold tried to awaken his students to awareness of social injustices in the world outside the school. To achieve this, he sought to curb selfishness, to reprove the wealthier boys for a habitual want of sympathy toward the lower classes, to inculcate "reverence for law and regard for the poor."[13] Arthur Hugh Clough's fictional Tory uncle in *Dipsychus* gruffly objected to Dr. Arnold's moralism: "How often have I not heard from you, how he used to attack offences, not as offences—the right view—against discipline, but as sin, heinous guilt, I don't know what beside! Why didn't he flog them and hold his tongue? Flog them he did, but why preach?"

All of Dr. Arnold's interests were reflected in his conduct of the school. "Whatever labour he bestowed on his literary works," said Dean Stanley, "was only part of that constant progress of self-education which he thought essential to the right discharge of his duties as a teacher. Whatever interest he felt in the struggles of the political and ecclesiastical world, reacted on his interest in the school, and invested it in his eyes with a new importance."[14] Like Thomas Carlyle, he enjoined and exemplified a gospel of work: "The precept flowed steadily from his life still more than from his lips, 'Work.' Not, work at this or that—but, Work."[15]

Characteristic of Dr. Arnold's humanitarian temper was his wish "to get up a real Poor Man's Magazine, which should not bolster up abuses and veil iniquities, nor prose to the poor as to children; but should address them in the *style* of Cobbett, plainly, boldly, and in sincerity, excusing nothing—concealing nothing—and misrepresenting nothing—but speaking the very whole truth

in love—Cobbett-like in style—but Christian in spirit."[16] Characteristic of his ecclesiastical liberalism was his recommendation
to admit Dissenters of all sects to preach in the pulpits of
parish churches, a proposal so appalling to the higher clergy
that it is said to have cost him a bishopric.[17] At a time when the
Duke of Wellington had recently defended in the House of
Lords the perfection of British parliamentary representation,
when Bishop Samuel Horsley said that he did not know what
the people of a country had to do with the laws except to obey
them, and when Earl Grey's first, and defeated, Reform Bill was
being debated in Commons, Dr. Arnold wrote of the bill to his
friend Baron von Bunsen, "I believe that, if it passes now, 'Felix
saeclorum nascitur ordo.' "[18] And characteristic too was his cultural ideal—"what is wanted is a deep knowledge and sympathy
with the European character and institutions."[19] These moral
and intellectual attitudes were not lost on Matthew Arnold, but
he became much more than "his father's forum"—to quote the
phrase of W. H. Auden's clever but deprecatory poem.

Arnold, with his brother Tom, was taught at home for some
years by Herbert Hill, a son-in-law of the poet Robert Southey;
and in August, 1836, he entered Winchester for a year.[20] He
began his career at Rugby in 1837; it was not highly distinguished. Mary Fletcher, a neighbor of the Arnolds at their
summer home Fox How, confided to her own mother: "I see that
our dear Mrs. Arnold's trials are to come from her sons. . . .
Matt's passion for fishing is as strong as Henry Fletcher's. He
is not to be allowed to go to College unless he shows a more
decided sense of duty in his school work the next half year."[21]
Arnold is reported, when standing behind his father's chair as
discipline at Rugby, to have diverted his schoolmates by making
faces from that vantage point. In 1840 he did win a prize at
Rugby for his poem *Alaric at Rome*; in the same year he was
awarded an open classical scholarship at Balliol and in 1841 a
scholarship from Rugby School.

Alaric at Rome was not quite Arnold's first literary effort. His
first "book," which H. F. Lowry has described, is supposed to
have been a precocious story, written at the age of seven, reflecting his reading of John Bunyan's *Pilgrim's Progress*.[22] His first
recorded poem, dated October 10, 1835, is a Latin tutorial ex-

ercise, a Horatian ode, on the occasion of the second birthday of his sister Frances—"Natalis dies Bonzensis."[23] Bonze was the name given to Frances, who, like the other children at Fox How, enjoyed canine nicknames (Jane was "K," Matthew—"Crab," Thomas—"Prawn"); and they followed kennel rules for behavior, rules devised to some extent as measures of safety in boating and swimming, but to some extent for parental convenience. For example: "VI. That no Dog cut chips in the Drawing or Dining Room, and that no Dog whatever do go into the kitchen or larder."[24]

Arnold's second known poem is "Lines Written on the Seashore at Eaglehurst, July 12, 1836."[25] These verses, written during a visit to an aunt on the Isle of Wight, are as full of Naiads and eighteenth-century diction as the birthday poem was inevitably furnished with Latin poetic tags, like *veloci pede* and *anni volucres. Alaric at Rome* is a great advance on these lines, but it is imitatively Byronic in sensibility and in theme, substantiating the appropriateness of the tone of romantic paradox expressed in its epigraph from *Childe Harold*: "Admire, exult, despise, laugh, weep, for here/There is such matter for all feeling."

Yet there are Arnoldian elements in *Alaric in Rome*—for example, the oblique approach to the theme; the conjectural thoughts for this meditative Alaric, which suggest the alternatives later devised for Mycerinus; the regret for "Energies wasted, unimproved hours"; and, as C. B. Tinker and H. F. Lowry note, the elegiac tone—"Tranquilly, above that troubled breast,/The sunny waters hold their joyous way"[26]—but there is little to anticipate the stylistic distinction of the best poems in the 1849 volume. *Alaric at Rome* was printed as a pamphlet at Rugby in 1840; Arnold himself never republished the poem.

II *Oxford*

Arnold was enrolled for entry at Balliol College on November 28, 1840. A classmate, Edward Walford, who matriculated on the same day, recalled that, as they waited in the Vice-Chancellor's ante-room, Arnold professed "his great aversion to sundry statements in the Thirty-nine Articles, which at that time we were all forced to subscribe, especially that article which expresses an approval of the Athanasian creed, and that which renounces the Pope of Rome." He may have disputed some of the articles, but he seems never to have agonized as did his friend Clough, who finally in 1852 resigned his Oriel fellowship because of scruples of religious conscience. Walford also recalled how, in his early days at Balliol when dining at the same table "in opposition to the Tractarianism of the day, he used to say that the strict imposition of creeds had done more to break up than to unite churches, and nations, and families, and how even then, in our small and highly privileged circle, he was the apostle of religious toleration in every direction."[27] He had indeed accepted the theological liberalism of his father, of whom John Henry Newman had gravely asked, "But is *he* a Christian?"

Before his matriculation at Oxford, Arnold had acquired an enthusiasm for travel that remained with him and an admiration for France that he displayed with some ostentation in his Oxford years. He had been in northern France with his parents in 1837, and he visited France again with his father and Tom in the spring of 1841. At Oxford he favored Pierre-Jean de Béranger among poets, George Sand among novelists. He affected dandified dress and a rather grand manner. Friedrich Max Müller, who came to Oxford in 1847 when Arnold had finished his undergraduate years at Balliol and was a fellow at Oriel, remembered his "Olympian manners." "The sound of his voice," he said, "and the wave of his arm were Jovelike."[28] The comment was made late in Arnold's Oxford years, but all reports confirm the impression of his consciously aloof demeanor. There is the amusing testimony of a poem by "K" in the January, 1842, number of the unpublished *Fox How Magazine*, which the young Arnolds devised for home consumption, about a "fine young Oxford gentleman" with eyeglass and a preoccupation with clothes and appearance:

> Eau de Mille Fleurs, Eau de Cologne and twenty eaux beside
> Rowland's Odonto, scented soaps, jostle his books aside.[29]

An early enthusiasm for fishing continued into Arnold's Oxford vacations, which some students devoted to study; and it continued throughout his life. "I came up here," he wrote in March,

1843, to John Duke Coleridge from Fox How, "in full expectation of being able to devote myself to the great delight of the year, fly-fishing; but we have had January weather, and the ground, last night and this morning, has been covered with snow. You cannot conceive the delight I find in my solitary fishing among the mountains here."[30]

The detached and airy manner of the undergraduate which disturbed some contemporaries enters engagingly into Arnold's early correspondence. The airiness at times took a patronizing manner effectively designed to needle the victim. In the summer of 1843, when Arnold was visiting his friend J. Manley Hawker in Devonshire, Hawker complained to John Duke Coleridge: "Arnold, at present, hardly acknowledges that there is anything to admire in the glorious scenery about here, and says that the hills are lumpy." And again he wrote Coleridge in exasperation: "I am fully prepared to do justice to Westmoreland, but I must confess that the one-sided views of our friend Matt. would urge one to retaliate in his own coin. It certainly is most trying to hear a man say of a country which you have for years been accustomed to admire in every shape and under every aspect, 'this is nice, *when* it has the sun upon it,' in a sort of patronising concession to me."[31] Arnold in the same summer, when urging Coleridge to come to Hawker's from Teignmouth before he himself returned to Fox How, wrote with the ironic gravity of his mature satiric vein:

See what it is to say rash things! I had quite forgotten my unfortunate assertion that Devonshire was overpraised, and you now bring it forward to throw suspicion on my judgment. But of my judgment I abate nothing. The rivers and valleys are fine, and Holme Chase is beautiful, but the hills seem to me to be worth very little, except for the sake of that sublimest of stones, granite, of which they are composed. But I must be altogether wrong about Devonshire—for dining, the other evening, with the Reverend Hamilton Southcombe, our curate, he and a man of the name of Grainger (so I took it) decided positively and authoritatively that Devonshire was pre-eminent in beauty among the English counties, and teemed with great men and remarked at the same time, with great force and shrewdness on the singular insensibility of Devonshire men to their own merits and their country's, and the very reprehensible silence they maintained on the subject. Undoubtedly they know, being Devonshire men, and so, of course, I must have been wrong.[32]

The outwardly exuberant manner and the banter may have made him something of a social lion; they may have achieved an objective in preserving the privacy requisite for nurturing the 1849 poems; but they also resulted in disconcerting at times even friends so intimate as Clough. Arnold found himself in the summer of 1844 explaining to J. D. Coleridge:

It is difficult for me to know in what terms to express myself after your last letter, so completely is it penetrated with that unfortunate error as to my want of interest in my friends which you say they have begun to attribute to me. It is an old subject which I need not discuss over again with you. The accusation, as you say, is not true. I laugh too much and they make one's laughter mean too much. However, the result is that when one wishes to be serious one cannot but fear a half suspicion on one's friends' part that one is laughing, and, so, the difficulty gets worse and worse.[33]

The numerous anecdotes concerning Arnold's Oxford years are both illuminating of his personality and in themselves diverting. They can be used to dramatize an image of a son diametrically opposed to a father who could be heavily earnest, austere, and autocratic. They show Arnold's deliberate intention to create a debonair manner to confront the world and a voice to lend persuasiveness to it. He was puzzling to acquaintances, even to friends. William Charles Lake, afterwards Dean of Durham, to whom as tutor both Matthew and Thomas Arnold were sent the summer before Matthew was elected scholar at Balliol, commented that with all his brilliance he was equally idle and desultory; and he regretted that his "want of knowledge of his books lost him his 'first'" when he took his degree at Balliol. Moreover, Lake reported that Arnold's tutors, particularly the lexicographer Liddell, were disappointed that he fell short of achieving the highest honors that his abilities promised.[34] Nevertheless, he won two scholarships to Balliol; he won in 1843 the prize for his poem *Cromwell*, the subject set by the university for that year; and, despite his graduation in 1844 with second-class honors, he earned a Fellowship at Oriel College in 1845.

Some verses written while he was an undergraduate, or within a few months of graduation, reveal the meditativeness that was as characteristic as the levity. These are an interesting twenty-line fragment beginning "Rude Orator," and the poems "Stagyrus" and "Shakespeare" of the 1849 volume. "Rude Orator" was first published in C. B. Tinker and H. F. Lowry's *The Poetry of Matthew Arnold: A Commentary*. The lines appear on a page of the Yale Manuscript bearing the date 1843, although the date suggests rather than proves the time of composition. The speaker of these melodramatic lines, who is quite conceivably a figure in an uncompleted dramatic monologue, protests the facile optimism of the "orator" about human happiness. On the contrary, he insists, though man is reason's heir, man has renounced that heritage; moreover, his own heart knows "such a damning catalogue of Ills," "such Instances/Raked from the swarming Gulf of Sorrow's Hell" as can controvert the specious argument. Stagyrus, to whom St. Chrysostom addressed a letter of counsel, was a young man possessed of a demon. In Arnold's poem—for the title may only be an afterthought as Kenneth Allott, as well as Tinker and Lowry, proposes—the young man in his litany begs the Word for the illumination that will relieve his pride and doubt and bring peace.[35]

The third poem, of the three, the only one of merit, is the sonnet to Shakespeare. The well-known line "Self-school'd, self-scann'd, self-honour'd, self-secure" makes the dramatist rather too much a Rugby product. However, it represents a Shakespeare detached, aloof, inscrutable, above the systems of morality that men clumsily derive from him, yet articulate for all the sufferings of mankind.[36] It gives a conception related to Keats's image of the Shakespeare that he characterized by "negative capability." But more important, the Shakespeare of this sonnet epitomizes what Arnold continuously sought: a sensibility that integrates the intellectual and passionate experience of humanity, a sensibility whose poised achievement is a *showing* of things as they are, uncontaminated by anxieties of a propagandistic kind.

There is a letter from Arnold to Clough that Lowry assigns to the spring of 1845 that bears on this point. Enthusiasm seems to have obscured Arnold's grammatical construction, but not his tenor. Apparently fearing contamination to George Sand's artistic integrity that may come with the spread of her fame, he says: "But never without a Pang do I hear of the growing Popularity of a strong minded writer. Then I know what hideosities what Solecisms, what Lies, what crudities, what distortions, what Grimaces, what affectations, what disown[m]ents of that Trimmer-X-Hannah-More-typed spirit they are of, I shall hear and see amongst the born-to-be-tight-laced of my friends and acquaintance: then I know the strong minded writer will lose his self-knowledge, and talk of his usefulness and imagine himself a Reformer, instead of an Exhibition."[37] "Exhibition" is an unhappy word, but for the moment it expressed the static quality of esthetic contemplation which, for Arnold the poet, is what poetry invites.

It is a great tribute to Dr. Arnold that he left his sons free to choose their careers "down to the very close of the years of education and preparation." "To the best of my belief," said his son Thomas, "he never thought of prescribing to him [Matthew] in any way either the field within which, or the aims towards which, he should set his genius to work."[38] Matthew Arnold found a resource in intellectual companionship, for he entered Oxford at a time lively with issues of political, economic, and social reform: Chartist agitation, the anti-Corn Law movement, factory legislation, Irish grievances. Oxford itself was animated by the Tractarian controversy that culminated when Newman left St. Mary's in 1843.

Arnold was a member of the Decade, a debating society (the Decayed, it was inevitably and facetiously called), which included J. D. Coleridge, Benjamin Jowett, Arthur Stanley, Clough, W. C. Lake, Frederick Temple, J. C. Shairp, and Theodore Walrond. They met in one another's rooms and "discussed all things human and divine." One member said, "We thought we stripped all things to the very bone, we believed we dragged recondite truths into the light of common day and subjected them to the scrutiny of what we were pleased to call our minds. We fought to the very stumps of our intellect."[39]

When Thomas Arnold joined his brother and Clough at Oxford in 1842, they formed with Walrond what Tom called "a little interior company."[40] They went skiffing together on the Cherwell; they breakfasted together on Sundays in Clough's rooms. "These were times," Tom said, "of great enjoyment. Sir Robert Peel was in power; he was breaking loose more and more from the trammels of mere party connexion, and the shrewd Rentoul, who then edited the *Spectator,* welcomed in the Conservative chief the only true statesman that England had seen since the days of Canning. The *Spectator* of the day before used to arrive at breakfast-time, and the leading articles were eagerly read and discussed."[41] Even in these years Arnold's intellectual interests were characteristically eclectic. The Epicurean Béranger remained a favorite with Matthew Arnold through the Oxford years (he found him somewhat *"fade"* by 1848).[42] Yet Goethe superseded Byron in Arnold's more serious poetical taste; Emerson's Transcendentalism engaged him; the style and the liberal humanitarian idealism of George Sand appealed strongly to him; he discovered the counsels to resignation in the *Bhagavad Gita;* and, his brother said, "the perfect handling of words, joined to the delicate presentation of ideas, attracted him powerfully to John Henry Newman, whose Sunday afternoon sermons at St. Mary's he for a long time regularly attended."[43] Thomas Arnold's daughter was, in a sense, correct when she said in her memoirs that Matthew Arnold was not touched "in the smallest degree by Newman's opinions";[44] but in later correspondence with Cardinal Newman, Arnold named Newman, Goethe, Wordsworth, and Sainte-Beuve as those from whom he had learned "habits, methods, ruling ideas, which are constantly with me."[45] But Arnold himself stayed outside the Tractarian controversy, at times an amused spectator of it, although his father, as well as academic Oxford, was deeply engaged in it.

If the Tractarian or Oxford movement had an official beginning, it was the sermon "National Apostasy," that John Keble delivered at St. Mary's, on July 14, 1833. Keble was protesting a proposal to secularize the revenues of certain bishoprics; he was protesting too against the liberal views of Dr. Arnold's *Principles of Church Reform* (1833) that minimized differences of denomination and dogma and that closely identified church and state. The rift widened between the Broad Church, latitudinarian Dr. Arnold and the saintly Keble, who had stood sponsor to Matthew Arnold at his baptism—Keble with his "Flibbertigibbet, fanatical, twinkling expression,"[46] his god-son once irreverently said. For the Tractarians' aim was, as Newman said in his *Apologia*, "to keep the Church from being liberalized." Yet to Dr. Arnold the doctrine of apostolic succession itself was "a profane heraldic theory."[47]

Antagonisms were sharpened by the publication in the *Edinburgh Review* in 1836 of an article attacking the Tractarians' opposition to an appointment to the Regius Professor of Divinity at Oxford. The article carried the acrimonious title, given it unfortunately by the editor of the *Review,* "The Oxford Malignants and Dr. Hampden."[48] Dr. Arnold's fitness to continue at Rugby was challenged; but he survived, and briefly triumphed. In August, 1841, shortly before the fall of Melbourne's Whig ministry, he was appointed to the Regius Chair of Modern History at Oxford; he delivered his inaugural lecture on December 2 in the great Clarendon Theatre. On June 12, 1842, the day before his forty-seventh birthday, he died at Rugby of angina pectoris.

The disappointment of Matthew Arnold's graduation from Balliol in 1844 with second-class honors was in some measure offset by his achieving election on March 28, 1845, to a fellowship at Oriel. Part of that interim was filled by teaching Classics in the fifth form at Rugby under his father's successor, Dr. A. C. Tait. The period was brief; our knowledge of it is largely apocryphal. Arthur Gray Butler, who had been at Rugby under Tait, when Matthew Arnold was temporarily an assistant-master, published in his late years a novel called *The Three Friends: a Story of Rugby in the Forties* (1900). In one scene in which he introduced Clough and Arnold, Butler seized on Arnold's insouciant and buoyant manner. Miss Fulton, who has just tabulated the grades for her brother who is a tutor, says: "I thought Tudor would come out first."

"Exactly," said Arnold, "That is just what I would do. Tudor is the first boy in the Form, I should say, and Tudor would appear first. And some other boys ought to be at the bottom-about a dozen of them," he added thoughtfully—"and they would come out bottom. And so justice would be done, and none of the bother!"

"But I assure you, Mr. Arnold, I added them up very carefully. I went over them twice."

"I am sure you did, Miss Fulton. And fancy and figures happily coincide. How delightful! But I must go. Amid the general decay of virtue at the present moment, let us not forget punctuality and the third lesson! Good-afternoon!"[49]

Butler's scene has the virtue of plausibility, especially in the light of the whimsical character in which Arnold presented himself to a correspondent in 1849: "I dined last night with a Mr. Grove, a celebrated man of science: his wife is pretty and agreeable, but not on a first interview. The husband and I agree wonderfully on some points. He is a bad sleeper, and hardly ever free from headache; he equally dislikes and disapproves of modern existence and the state of excitement in which everybody lives: and he sighs after a paternal despotism and the calm existence of a Russian or an Asiatic."[50]

In the interim before his return to Oxford Arnold began the remarkable correspondence with Arthur Hugh Clough, one that remains the best introduction to Arnold's personality and intellectual life. One fine satirical letter to Clough precedes the Oriel appointment; Arnold says, ". . . I do not give satisfaction at the Masters Meetings. For the other day when Tait had well observed that strict Calvinism devoted 1000s of mankind to be eternally—and paused—I, with, I trust, the True Xtian Simplicity suggested '——.' "[51] And in a vein of Falstaffian euphuism he sighed his dissatisfaction:

"But to be listless when you should be on Fire: to be full of headaches when you should slap your Thigh: to be rolling Paper Balls when you should be weaving fifty Spirits into one: to be raining when you had been better thundering: to be damped with a dull ditchwater, while in one school near you sputters and explodes a fiery tailed Rocket, and in the rest patent Simulators ceaselessly revolve: to be all this, and to know it—O my Clough—, in this house they find the Lodger in Apricot Marmalade for two meals a day—and yet?"[52]

Arnold was saved by the Oriel fellowship from teaching young scholars; however, fate ironically cast him for thirty-five years in a restrictive career as one of Her Majesty's Inspectors of Schools. Within the limits of fate, he exhibited what freedom he could. To the end of his life temperament and choice led him to instruct his fellow countrymen in the conduct of life with instruments of satire and of persuasion.

CHAPTER 2

"The Tragic Imperatives"

MATTHEW Arnold's residence at Oriel ended in the spring of 1846.[1] Thereafter he was at liberty to travel abroad in the long summer vacation, and in August he made a worshipful, sentimental journey to the scenes of the lyrical, early novels of George Sand. From Boussac he sent her a letter, "conveying to her, in bad French, the homage of a youthful and enthusiastic foreigner who had read her works with delight." In response she invited him to a mid-day breakfast at the Château de Nohant, where Chopin was among those present. "She made me sit by her," Arnold recalled, "and poured out for me the insipid and depressing beverage, *boisson fade et mélancolique,* as Balzac called it, for which English people are thought abroad to be always thirsting,—tea."[2] John Morley in later years repeated to Arnold a comment that George Sand had made to Ernest Renan. She said that Arnold had made on her the impression of a young Milton on his travels.

Ultimately Arnold's enthusiasm for George Sand moderated. In Paris in 1859, for example, he was disinclined, in spite of Sainte-Beuve's advice, " 'to take so long a journey to see such a fat old Muse,' as M. de Circourt says in his funny English."[3] Nevertheless, in still later years he assured his sister Fan that "she was the greatest spirit in our European world from the time that Goethe departed."[4] Following George Sand's death in 1876, he paid her the tribute of a thoughtfully appreciative essay in John Morley's *Fortnightly Review* (June, 1877); and, in the last year of his life, stimulated by her published correspondence, he considered writing a second essay on her.

In the *Fortnightly* essay Arnold did not attempt to recreate what he was thirty years earlier, but the tenor of his correspondence, as well as the themes and the attitudes expressed in his public essays and poetry, leave no doubt about the force on him of what he defined as "the principal elements" in her: "the cry of agony and revolt, the trust in nature and beauty, the aspiration towards a purged and renewed human society."[5] The aspiration toward a "social new-birth" was not lost on this son of Dr. Arnold. Although Matthew mocked Clough's hope for sudden social regeneration in 1848, the crowded year of European revolutions, his own chief concern from 1853 to 1888 was what he called "the society of the future." Besides the elements in George Sand already named, others clearly made their appeal. The cry of Jacques, "Life is arid and terrible . . . ; there is but one virtue, the eternal sacrifice of oneself";[6] the insistence on a human concern with life, not death;[7] and the ultimate sense that joy is necessary to a fruitful existence—these are major themes that recur in Arnold's poems and essays; but in 1846 joy was not yet a stated principle of his conduct of life. Essentially, Arnold treats George Sand as a moralist, not as a novelist. As a moralist, she is a source of numerous meditations, sentimental, stoical, humanitarian, in Arnold's *Note-Books* from 1856 to 1886.

In 1846, however, Arnold had other sentimental interests in France besides George Sand. In July he appears to have seen twice in London the great tragic actress Elisa Félix Rachel. One of her performances was in Racine's *Phèdre*. ". . . I followed her to Paris," he wrote, "and for two months never missed one of her representations."[8] He went to Paris on December 29, 1846, where he saw Rachel perform at least ten times. "She began almost where Mdlle. Sarah Bernhardt ends," he said years later; and, elaborating his comparison, he explained, ". . . I had never till now comprehended how much of Rachel's superiority was purely in intellectual power, how eminently this power counts in the actor's art as in all art, how just is the instinct which led the Greeks to mark with a high and severe stamp the Muses."[9] This idea of the austerity of art is implicit in the conception of the poet's role expressed in Arnold's early poems, such as the sonnet "To a Friend," "Resignation," and "The Strayed Reveller."

Arnold returned to Oxford in February, 1847, where he resumed his external, dandified gaiety. Clough wrote from Oriel to his sister Anne on the fifteenth: ". . . Matt Arnold is full of Paris and the things of Paris—specially the theatres." And on the twenty-second, in a letter to John Campbell Shairp, he amplified: ". . . Matt is full of Parisianism; theatres in general, and Rachel in special: he enters the room with a chanson of Béranger's on his lips—for the sake of French words almost conscious of tune: his carriarge shows him in fancy parading the rue de Rivoli;— and his hair is guiltless of English scissors: he breakfasts at twelve, and never dines in Hall, and in the week or 8 days rather (for 2 Sundays must be included) he has been to Chapel *once. . . ."*[10]

The return to Oxford was brief; for in April, 1847, Matthew Arnold became secretary to the aging Lord Lansdowne, president of the council in Lord John Russell's cabinet.[11] "My man," as Arnold in his letters to Clough facetiously calls him, was Henry Petty-Fitzmaurice, third Marquis of Lansdowne. He had entered political life in 1802 at the age of twenty-two as member of Parliament for Calne. On many issues his attitudes were like those of his friend, Dr. Arnold. He supported William Wilberforce in his efforts to abolish the slave trade; he advocated the removal of political disabilities for Jews; he supported Roman Catholic emancipation; and he supported Earl Grey on the issue of the Reform Bill of 1832.

Lord Lansdowne, who had been made president of the council on national education in 1833, was in addition a collector of works of art and a patron of men of letters, especially those of Whig persuasion, like Thomas Moore and Sydney Smith. His country house at Bowood Park in Wiltshire and Lansdowne House in London were, like Holland House, centers of Whig political life. The youthful Macaulay's ebullient account, beginning in the style of German Romantic melodrama, on his entrance into Holland House in 1831, is one of the memorable episodes in his biography. Arnold's letter of February 8, 1848, to his brother in New Zealand, at the outset of the third French revolution, equals it for a sense of the dramatic moment and for the irreverence of its mockery:

My Dearest Tom,— . . . Here I sit, opposite a marble group of Romulus and Remus and the wolf; the two children fighting like mad, and the limp-uddered she-wolf affectionately snarling at the little demons struggling on her back. Above it is a great picture, Rembrandt's Jewish Exiles, which would do for Consuelo and Albert resting in one of their wanderings, worn out upon a wild stormy heath sloping to the Baltic—she leaning over her two children who sleep in their torn rags at her feet. Behind me a most musical clock, marking now 24 Minutes past 1 P.M. On my left two great windows looking out on the court in front of the house, through one of which gushes the soft damp breath, with a tone of spring-life in it, which the close of an English February sometimes brings. . . . And from the square and the neighbouring streets, through the open door whereat the civil porter moves to and fro, come the sounds of vehicles and men, in all gradations, but mellowed by the time they reach this backstanding lordly mansion.

But above all cries come whereat every stone in this and all the other lordly mansions may totter and quake for fear:

> "Se—c—ond Edition of the Morning
> *Herald*—L—a—test news from Paris:—
> arrival of the King of the French."

I have gone out and bought the same portentous *Herald*, and send it herewith that you may read and know. As the human race forever stumbles up its great steps, so it is now.[12]

The interest of the letter is divided between Arnold's amused regard for the setting of which he is so self-consciously a part and his assumed detachment towards the historic event of which he is the spectator. While the final phrase of the letter mocks the inadequacy of the cliché to express the course of humanity, Arnold seriously rejects the easy optimism that supposes that a golden age will return "at a human nod."

"If it were not for all these blessed revolutions, I should sink into hopeless lethargy,"[13] Clough wrote to J. C. Shairp. On the other hand, Arnold admired France for what he called her "civility" and for her achievements in the world of ideas. "France, famed in all great arts, in none supreme,"[14] he ungallantly described her in a sonnet to Clough. He explained to "K" that it was the *"intelligence* of their idea-moved masses" that puts France *"politically* in the van of Europe."[15] Yet he was fearful of the example of revolutionary France for an England whose deeply ignorant middle and upper classes lacked vision, whose masses would be moved, he thought, only to plunder and destroy. And the 1848 revolution in France was the impetus for renewed

Chartist activity in England; Arnold attended a Chartist meeting in April of that year, and was impressed by the ability of the speakers. "However," he commented, "I should be sorry to live under their government—nor do I intend to—though Nemesis would rejoice at their triumph."[16] Arnold facetiously addressed a letter to "Citizen Clough, Oriel Lyceum, Oxford";[17] and he privately challenged Clough's Utopian social and political hopes in his correspondence of 1848: "If there is necessity anywhere, it is in the Corruption of man, as Tom might say, only."[18] He thought momentarily of doing some political writing, but felt "no profound stirring"; and he challenged Clough's revolutionary enthusiasm publicly in the two sonnets "To a Republican Friend, 1848":

> this earth, whereon we dream,
> Is on all sides o'ershadow'd by the high
> Uno'erleaped Mountains of Necessity,
> Sparing us narrower margin than we deem.[19]

The phrase "the Corruption of man," which Tom Arnold might have used, carried with it for his brother the *odium theologicum* that prevented Matthew's own unqualified use of it. Instead he used, in his poem "Resignation," the phrase, "the something that infects the world," to express his own sense of a cosmic source for human disquietude. "Would that I were coming home," he wrote from Lansdowne House to "K" at Fox How. "It is so hard to sequester oneself here from the rush of public changes and talk, and yet so unprofitable to attend to it." He ended his letter despairingly, "Be kind to the neighbours, 'this is all we can.' "[20]

In Homer, Epictetus, Sophocles, Lucretius, Goethe, Senancour, Arnold was finding lessons of detachment and endurance; in Carlyle and Emerson, refreshment from "the hot dizzy trash" of popular journalism. And he was discovering the relevance to his situation of the philosophy of the *Bhagavad Gita* with its counsel to renounce the subjective life to win a purer contemplation.[21] "I am disappointed," he told Clough in March, 1848, "the Oriental wisdom, God grant it were mine, pleased you not."[22] Arnold's conception of the individual human condition is essentially defined by the volume of poems that his leisure as Lord

Lansdowne's secretary enabled him to prepare for the press during 1848. On February 26, 1849, *The Times* advertised for sale *The Strayed Reveller, and Other Poems,* published in London by B. Fellowes.[23] The identity of the author was disguised under the initial "A."

I *The Strayed Reveller*

Arnold told his sister "K" soon after the book appeared that he felt "rather as a reformer in poetical matters. . . . If I have health & opportunity to go on," he said, "I will shake the present methods until they go down, see if I don't. More and more I feel bent against the modern English habit (too much encouraged by Wordsworth) of using poetry as a channel for thinking aloud, instead of making anything."[24]

The poems in the book exemplify Arnold's chief devices for "making," including notably, though not exclusively, the symbolic use of myth. In form, he favors the dramatic or lyric monologue, soliloquy, narrative, and the more immediately personal sonnet. The poems express the ideal vision of the poet, man's confrontation by forces of alien nature, his moral consciousness, the elements of flux and constancy in the life of man and nature, and the imperfectness of human sympathies. They reveal an inquiring and skeptical intelligence deeply concerned with humanistic values of mankind, and with the spiritual alienation and emotional isolation of the individual. These themes, sometimes touched more fully in later poems, are broached in these poems in an often arresting way.

The title poem, "The Strayed Reveller," relates dramatically a brief confrontation of Circe, Ulysses, and a follower of Bacchus to express the isolation of the poet. The setting of this idyll, which Arnold handles in the free-verse form that he knew through Heine and Goethe, is the porch of Circe's palace at evening, to which the young reveller has wandered. The relationship between Ulysses and Circe is more akin to the intelligent, mature emotion that attached Shakespeare's Theseus to Hippolyta than to anything in the Homeric myth. For, while Ulysses remains a Homerically "dark-featured,/Quick-eyed stranger," he is no more wily and devious than Tennyson's Ulysses; and Arnold's statuesque Circe has more of the enchantment, and compassionateness, of a muse of poetry than the allure of a sensual sorceress. Perhaps she is the imaginative power of apprehending life that stimulates the poet.

The poem deals with modes of seeing human experience. It may be surveyed firsthand, practically but unreflectively, as by Ulysses; it may be seen comprehensively but indifferently, at no emotional cost, as by the deities; or it may be imaginatively known by the poet in all its existential modes, but it is comprehended by him only at the price of suffering with his creations. The experience of the poet is more godlike than that of Ulysses, being more comprehensive in time and space. Yet

> The Gods are happy.
> They turn on all sides
> Their shining eyes.[25]

The "wise bards" suffer. They must feel the passions they represent. Their wisdom *is* their beholding, not the meaning of what they see. To the seeing poet, like Tiresias, the Gods

> Added this law:
> That they should bear too
> His groping blindness,
> His dark foreboding,
> His scorn'd white hair.

"'. . . the Muse,'" Arnold wrote to Clough, "'willingly *accompanies* life but . . . in no wise does she understand to *guide* it.'"[26] The Strayed Reveller has not yet learned this lore himself; he has only heard it from Silenus. What he has seen, he has seen "without pain, without labour." But he has seen only a fragment of human experience:

> Sometimes a wild-hair'd Maenad—
> Sometimes a Faun with torches—
> And sometimes, for a moment,
> Passing through the dark stems
> Flowing-robed, the beloved,
> The desired, the divine,
> Beloved Iacchus.

The last lines of the poem confront the Reveller with a choice: to rest content with his fragmentary emotional experience and the lore of Silenus at second hand, or to fulfill his power to be a poet, accepting the human price. He chooses Circe's cup again. Her cup is not Keats's beaker full of the warm South; it is the imaginative force that will permit him to know the "bright procession" of human experience. He does not escape experience; he asks to be invaded by it:

> Faster, faster,
> O Circe, Goddess,
> Let the wild, thronging train,
> The bright procession
> Of eddying forms,
> Sweep through my soul!

Experience, even in the case of this Reveller, who reflects Arnold's sensibility, is not gained by a Faust-like dedication of oneself to turbulence. Arnold thought it a limitation of Robert Browning even in the 1840's that he desired movement and fullness, and so obtained only "a confused multitudinousness." Arnold insisted to Clough that one "must begin with an Idea of the world in order not to be prevailed over by the world's multitudinousness: or if they cannot get that, at least with isolated ideas: and all other things shall (perhaps) be added unto them."[27] One must achieve the detachment of Shakespeare, or of Homer, Epictetus, and Sophocles, whom Arnold praised in his famous sonnet "To a Friend."

The ideas of the world that Arnold began with are sobering ones. Like Wordsworth's conjecture about the possibility of prenatal existence in his "Ode on the Intimations of Immortality," the ideas Arnold shaped into poems are only hypotheses, passionately felt, not points of faith. Yet, as the product of one man thinking, they have a consistency of temper. Not unreasonably did Arnold later object to those who "calmly say, dropping all mention of the real speakers, 'Mr. Arnold here professes his Pantheism,' or 'Mr. Arnold here disowns Christianity.'"[28] The ideas about the world of nature external to man express his alienation from it, as shown in "Quiet Work," "In Harmony with Nature," and "In Utrumque Paratus."

In the sonnet "Quiet Work," which seems to owe more to Plotinus's thought than to Goethe's, with which it has sometimes been associated, the processes of nature are emblematic of an ideal of activity performed in tranquility that man might emulate; but the processes are only there, outside of man; they do not relate to him in a transcendental way, as in Wordsworth, nor do they impinge on his religious sense, even rationalistically, like Addison's "spacious firmament on high." And in the impatient sonnet "In Harmony with Nature," which in 1849 was called "To an Independent Preacher, who preached that we should be 'In Harmony with Nature,'" Arnold declares that Nature is cruel, stubborn, fickle, exacting. Nature is divorced from the moral sense: "Man must begin, know this, where Nature ends." The dilemma resembles that proposed by Fulke Greville in the grand chorus of his *Mustapha,*

> Oh, wearisome condition of humanity,
> Born under one law, to another bound;
> Vainly begot, and yet forbidden vanity,
> Created sick, commanded to be sound.

The alternative views of man's origin, for which Arnold's "In Utrumque Paratus" enjoins us to be prepared, combine with his unallied existence to tell us that his dearest conceptions are subjective and illusory. Whether the world originates as the projection of a divine mind, or as the product of chance and matter, man has no ground for pride.

The forlornness, the alienation of the individual, and his ultimate sense of his limitations in a world he never made find a symbol in the early stanzas "To a Gipsy Child by the Sea-Shore." The child conveys to the poet profound intimations of man's mortality, and he also intimates alternative ways of confronting this awareness. As did Lear, man may bear the majesty of grief that he has learned in the world of new experience; or his reason may lead him to surmise the nature of his fate and, achieving a stoic calm, to "Stand mute, self-centred, stern, and dream no more."[29] Stoic calm is also enjoined in "The World and the Quietist," which reflects Arnold's enthusiasm—and Clough's reservations—for the counsel to passiveness of the *Bhagavad Gita.* And the gnomic Chorus, which speaks compassionately but unflinchingly in the "Fragment of an 'Antigone,'" recalls the myths of Eos and Ajax to subdue and instruct the passionately suffering Haemon, if by example he will be instructed and subdued.

Man's plight in an indifferent world, where necessity and chance operate, arises from his own humanity, from his sense of justice and his sense of compassion. For example, in "Mycerinus" a subjective sense of what is right and just is outraged by fact. In "The Sick King in Bokhara" compassionateness comes in conflict with both an obsolete code of punishment and a human wish to atone one's guilt. The idealistic heroine of George Sand's novel *Lélia*, Arnold reminds us, divined the suffering of mankind from the time of Prometheus onward; and, for answer to her protest against injustice, she only heard "the despairing sob of impotent agony."[30] Her cries for *Truth!* have only been mocked through the ages by infinite space answering *Desire*. Like Haemon, Mycerinus, and the modern Mohammedan King, man must learn, if he can, to endure a suffering inherent in the course of things.

In Arnold's poem, Mycerinus, king of Egypt, has lived virtuously and ruled well; his father Cheops's rule was notoriously unjust. Cheops enjoyed a long and happy life; Mycerinus is allotted six years of rule by the Gods. In Herodotus's story, Mycerinus's virtue is a fault, for he has obstructed a prophecy that Egypt would suffer for a hundred and fifty years. As Arnold retells the story, it is closer to the problem of Job, as Douglas Bush has observed;[31] but, for Mycerinus, there is no Lord to whom to submit, nor is there a restitution of goods at the end. Arnold's angry young king asks of what use is renunciation if there is no reward. Are the Gods indifferent to man, are they overruled by some Force, or are they, he asks with Lucretian overtones, in fact oblivious of man? With a final burst of sarcasm he cries,

> The will
> Of the great Gods is plain, and ye must bring
> Ill deeds, ill passions, zealous to fulfil
> Their pleasure, to their feet; and reap their praise,
> The praise of Gods, rich boon! and length of days.

He withdraws from his people to devote six years to revelry.

In what mood did Mycerinus spend those years, Arnold asks. The serenity of Arnold's concluding description suggests the preferred answer. Mycerinus, he tells us, "bent his way/ To the cool region of the groves he loves"; and he tells how "the deep-burnish'd foliage overhead/ Splinter'd the silver arrows of the moon." Language and rhythm temper our sense of the bacchanalian riotousness of the feast, and they weigh visibly on the side of a stoic choice the seeming equal alternatives that are proposed: perhaps Mycerinus spent six years in a hedonism only occasionally disturbed by a *memento mori*; perhaps behind the mask of hedonism he day by day grew stronger in stoic calm.

In "The Sick King in Bokhara" the malady of the King is less the fever that afflicts his city, than the merciful humanitarianism of his conscience which conflicts with both the abstract justice of the community and the desire of the guilty individual to expiate his guilt. The King is one of the "impassioned seekers of a new and better world"[32] who fails. A man of Bokhara in a time of fever and drought has secretly filled his pitcher at a little pool and hidden it behind the door of his house. His mother and his brothers drain it during the sultry night:

> Now mark! I, being fever'd, sick
> (Most unblest also), at that sight
> Brake forth, and cursed them—and dost hear?—
> One was my mother—Now, do right!

The man demands the law—death by stoning. Reluctantly, the King, advised by the interpreters of the law, casts the first stone softly, "—but the man/ With a great joy upon his face,/ Kneel'd down, and cried not, neither ran." The man dies praising Allah. The young, compassionate King now sees that he is bound by a rule stronger than himself. He recognizes ways in which individual desire is circumscribed; and he commemorates his instinct for mercy by burying the man in the royal tomb:

> Bring water, nard, and linen rolls!
> Wash off all blood, set smooth each limb!
> Then say: "He was not wholly vile,
> Because a king shall bury him."

In their *The Poetry of Matthew Arnold: A Commentary*, Tinker and Lowry propose that Arnold illustrates in this poem "the supremacy of the law over the caprice of royal inclination."[33] This reading is difficult to share—just as it is difficult to share their seeing in "The Fragment of an 'Antigone'" a discussion of "the law of the family as opposed to selfish hedonism,"[34] the hedonist being Antigone's bereft lover. In "The Sick King in Bokhara" the speeches of the old Vizier and the young King that close the poem balance the issue in characteristically Arnoldian way. Their conflicting responses at first seem drawn, for the conclusion is not moralized by the poet, but left in suspense. The Vizier persuasively adduces, to moderate the King's passionate sympathy, examples of injustice in the world beyond the King's sphere of control which he must therefore endure; and he appeals to an obligation to maintain the law, however harsh. Yet the Vizier's final words are designed to elicit from the reader an adverse response to his hard indifferences:

> There are the lepers, and all sick;
> There are the poor, who faint alway.
>
> All these have sorrow, and keep still,
> Whilst other men make cheer, and sing.
> Wilt thou have pity on all these?
> No, nor on this dead dog, O King!

The Vizier, who began like a wise Creon, ends with the harshness of a Shylock. The Vizier's argument for punishing the man who requires his punishment may have strength on psychological grounds, like those that compel the Ancient Mariner in Coleridge's poem or Raskolnikov in Dostoevski's *Crime and Punishment*. But the Vizier is not aware of the psychology in the situation; he is only insistent upon the inexorableness of tribal law. The King, on the other hand, who has the final lines of the poem, seeks a more humane world. He gains in dignity by his thoughtful response to the Vizier's contempt; by his willingness to be tutored; and, above all, by his pity for mankind, as embodied in a "sinner." The dialectic of the poem favors the position of the young King. Yet the King's lesson is austere. He must seek; he also must suffer, and he must endure.

"The Fragment of an 'Antigone'" likewise presents two points of view. The issue is not a dilemma arising from a conflict of reasonable claims, but from a conflict between what the heart wishes and what fate imposes. The "fragment" is of course not a fragment, just as the later poem "Sohrab and Rustum, An Episode" is not a part of a larger whole but a form in itself. The opening Chorus praises two modes of conduct: first the man who, within the bounds of what is just, challenges fortune and seizes what happiness he can gain; second, the man who lives closely circumscribed by country, kindred, home. The Chorus next describes the chances they "Must every day endure:/ Voyages, exiles, hates, dissensions, wars" and "Death, who dissevers all." It continues:

> Him then I praise, who dares
> To self-selected good
> Prefer obedience to the primal law,
> Which consecrates the ties of blood; for these, indeed,
> Are to the Gods a care;
> That touches but himself.

These lines praise the individual who, like Antigone, finds scope for action in the second line of conduct rather than the first. Haemon enters bitterly lamenting that Antigone, honoring her dead brother in preference to a lover, is more cruel than Creon, whom he does not blame. The Chorus replies that even the Dawn-Goddess could not save Orion from the eternal law of death, that even Zeus acquiesced at last in the fate of his son Heracles.

The "Fragment" exists, not to blame Haemon as a selfish hedonist, but to present the poignancy of his situation. Like the King in Bokhara, like Mycerinus, he must choose. His choice is between fruitlessly chafing against facts that confront him, and bearing the fact with the quiet and knowing fortitude that the Chorus itself exemplifies.

Death separates Haemon and Antigone, but there are, however, other modes of severance that interested Arnold. Imperfect sympathies, arising from differences subtly psychological in their origin, provide themes for "A Modern Sappho" and "The

Forsaken Merman" in the 1849 volume, just as they find expression subsequently in the poems that comprise "Switzerland" and in "Tristram and Iseult." Moreover, all readers of Arnold will remember that the possibility of the rare actuality of full emotional sympathy affords the sole point of stability in the insecure world of "Dover Beach."

Arnold found in the Danish legend of the love of a Merman and a mortal woman a congenial myth to express the inexorable force of imperfect sympathies in "The Forsaken Merman." Margaret, having lived with the Merman, returns to her native home on Easter Day, choosing, we suppose, the country, kinsfolk, and home that the Chorus of the "Fragment of an 'Antigone'" had praised. Yet her recognition of her irresolvably divided sympathies on the one hand, and the fidelity and pathos of the Merman and his children, on the other, for all their alien world, hold in close balance the reader's response. For the clear green sea, the cool deep caverns, and red-gold throne of their fantastic world contrast to some advantage with Margaret's pallid world of white and grey, of graves and church and rain. Arnold's achievement is not to invite censure or approval. With ironic detachment, rather like Flaubert's, he objectifies the sad discrepancy between what is fated and what is desired.

The final poem of *The Strayed Reveller, and Other Poems* is "Resignation." Interestingly, if not altogether persuasively, it has been examined as a reply to Wordsworth's "Lines Written a Few Miles above Tintern Abbey," but the parallels and contrasts should alert readers of Arnold's poetry to avoid confusing his attitude toward man's relations with external nature with Wordsworth's attitude.[35] The most "Wordsworthian" of Arnold's poems are the sonnets, which, like "Written in Butler's Sermons," "Written in Emerson's Essays," or "Religious Isolation," have the dogmatic and indignantly righteous tone of some of Wordsworth's so-called patriotic sonnets. The "nature" poems of Arnold are only superficially Wordsworthian, as in some aspects of the pastoralism of setting. External nature for Arnold never has a Transcendental spiritual connection with man. Wordsworth frequently uses words like "interfuse" and "intertwine," with their important metaphysical implications, to suggest this connection. But these terms are not elements in Arnold's poetical vocabulary;

for him "the primrose by the river's brim" was, quite satisfactorily, a yellow primrose.

"Resignation" is a monologue addressed to Fausta, presumably Arnold's sister "K." We infer that, like Goethe's Faust, she interpreted the Word of St. John as *activity*, and that she wished, like Faust, restlessly to engage in a world of constant motion and, thus absorbed, to avoid confrontation with its meaning. The speaker in the poem addresses her as they return after ten years to climb in the Lake Country. In this pastoral setting the relative permanence of the natural world contrasts with the human world of busy change. A band of gipsies in the poem, however, suggests man's capacity to approximate in his own habits the quietude of nature's processes. At their primitive level, the gipsies, acquiescent and enduring, contrast with the vivid sensibility of the poetic temperament as well as with the life of Faustlike activity.

For the poet of "Resignation," like the Strayed Reveller, comprehends—in the life of imagination, not of action—all the experience of mankind. "Not deep the poet sees, but wide," the speaker imagines Fausta to say. She echoes Goethe's remark that "the great point with the poet is to express a manifold world." Although the gipsies are less sensitive, and the poet more sensitive than the common man, both teach that they "who await/ No gifts from chance, have conquered fate." The speaker discerns in the quiet work of nature a lesson enjoining detachment and resignation, "a sad lucidity of soul," a withdrawal of self to participate in "the general life." In the final injunction to Fausta, the speaker not only reiterates the lesson of resignation in so many poems of this volume, but he also raises an issue that Arnold never explored, although he hinted at it in some of his poems. He discerns a metaphysical evil as a source of man's alienation from his environment, as a source of a malaise that is not attributable to death or chance:

> The solemn hills around us spread,
> This stream which falls incessantly,
> The strange-scrawl'd rocks, the lonely sky,
> If I might lend their life a voice,
> Seem to bear rather than rejoice.

> And even could the intemperate prayer
> Man iterates, while these forbear,
> For movement, for an ampler sphere,
> Pierce Fate's impenetrable ear;
> Not milder is the general lot
> Because our spirits have forgot,
> In action's dizzying eddy whirl'd,
> The something that infects the world.

In the poem "On First Looking into Loeb's Horace," Lawrence Durrell defines what he calls "the tragic imperatives": "Seek, suffer, endure." These Classical injunctions form the counsel that Arnold also perceived in George Sand from Homer, from Sophocles, from Epictetus. They express the tenor of the greater part of the human experience that Arnold explores in the poems that he published in 1849; indeed, they form the burden of the greater part of the human experience he treats in all his poetry.

The best of Arnold's poetry expresses dilemmas of the mind and heart, not solutions; it is the merit of the poems that we experience the anxiety of the dilemma. In his prose work, Arnold is committed and actively seeks solutions; but there is a continuity in these areas of his writing, for in both poetry and prose Arnold is concerned with morality. His prose is highly complex in its stylistic devices, and it takes many forms. But in the large perspective we see that he is continuously a moralist; he is in the tradition of Sir Philip Sidney, Sir Thomas Browne, and Dr. Samuel Johnson. As H. V. Routh once remarked with very great astuteness, "Arnold wrote as a moralist but did not escape being taken for a critic."[36]

CHAPTER 3

The Inspector of Schools

I *Winds of Change*

SOON after publication of *The Strayed Reveller, and Other Poems* James Anthony Froude confided to Clough: "I admire Matt— to a very great extent. Only I don't see what business he has to parade his calmness and lecture us on resignation when he has never known what a storm is, and doesn't know what he has to resign himself to—I think he only knows the shady side of nature out of books—."[1] The final comment may seem unfair, since the force of Arnold as a poet for modern readers lies in his power to imagine circumstances, especially those that represent the human condition and the limits of self-knowledge in a culture that was becoming increasingly materialized and secularized.

It is true that he did not know public storms of the kind Froude had just undergone. Clough, aware of his inability to subscribe to the Articles of the Church of England, had resigned his Oriel fellowship in 1848; Froude resigned his fellowship in 1849 under highly dramatic conditions. James Anthony Froude, like his older brother Hurrell, had originally been drawn at Oxford to the Tractarians; but, unlike the ascetic Hurrell, he had found them wanting. He discovered in the heterodox faith of Carlyle and in agnosticism more of the spirit of the age. His skeptical novel *The Nemesis of Faith* was advertised for sale within two days of publication of *The Strayed Reveller*. On February 27, 1849, William Sewell publicly burned a copy of *The Nemesis of Faith* at Exeter College, Oxford, of which Froude was a fellow. He was preached against in chapel, denounced in Hall.[2] He resigned his fellowship, a step already decided upon; and in addition he resigned his new appointment as headmaster of a high school in Tasmania.

Although Arnold had not faced so public a crisis, he felt the winds of controversy; and his inner life was deeply touched by his own sense of the inhospitableness of his times for poetry and of the difficulty of achieving his own identity in the welter of conflicting ideas and revolutionary change. His brother Tom recalled 1848 as a "time of boundless excitement" with Chartist meetings, barricades in Paris, Italy and Hungary fighting for national independence, Rome becoming a republic.[3] Matthew Arnold reacted to the currents of change, but he did not share the exhilaration. His "buried" life was more immediately touched by personal issues, for in the summer of 1848 he experienced the emotions that were crystalized in the "Marguerite" poems. He admitted in the autumn of that year to "a strong disposition to intellectual seclusion," a wish to find his own emotional and intellectual center.[4] While Arnold thought of his friend Clough as poking, patching, and cobbling in anxiety to find his center, he himself was taking the counsel enjoined in his own lines: "Resolve to be thyself; and know that he,/ Who finds himself, loses his misery!"

He was alienated for a time even from Clough—although he had thought of them in March, 1848, as "agreeing like two lambs in a world of wolves."[5] Irritated by a visit he made to Oxford in November, soon after the publication of Clough's poem *The Bothie of Tober-na-Vuosich*, Arnold wrote to Clough that he could, if need be, dispense with all his friends even Clough: "better that, than be sucked for an hour even into the Time Stream in which they and he [W. Y. Sellar] plunge and bellow."[6] "I became more calm in spirit, but uncompromising, almost stern," he continued; and, turning to Étienne Senancour's melancholy, introspective novel *Obermann*, he "refuged" himself, he said, "with him in his forest against your Zeit Geist."[7]

But the emotional residue of the sentimental, personal experience of which the "Switzerland" poems remain a partial record, and the pressures for change within the age penetrated the stoical solitude he imagined as his refuge. In September, 1849, he wrote again from Switzerland, where he had met "Marguerite," in a climactic exclamation of self-revealing and embittered disillusionment: "My dearest Clough these are damned times—everything is against one—the height to which

knowledge is come, the spread of luxury, our physical enervation, the absence of great *natures*, the unavoidable contact with
millions of small ones, newspapers, cities, light profligate friends,
moral desperadoes like Carlyle, our own selves, and the sickening
consciousness of our difficulties: but for God's sake let us neither
be fanatics nor yet chalf blown by the wind. . . ."[8]

Arnold's letters in this period record not only his turmoil but
also his power of self-analysis and his ability, ultimately, to
stake out his own line of endeavor. Those who see Arnold as
"harried" in conscience throughout his life by a God-Father
image and as burying his talent in deference to it read the evidence too subjectively. They overlook his capacity to make,
however painfully, his analysis of himself, even when forced to
the recognition "I am fragments"; and they overlook his freedom
to shape his own career.[9] But, whatever Arnold's inner perturba-
tions, he displayed outwardly as Lord Lansdowne's secretary the
familiar buoyancy. His disconcerting bearing is reflected in an
amusingly disapproving account of him by Charlotte Brontë:
"Striking and prepossessing in appearance, his manner displeases
from its seeming foppery. I own it caused me at first to regard
him with regretful surprise: the shade of Dr. Arnold seemed to
me to frown on his young representative. Ere long a real modesty
appeared under his assumed conceit, and genuine intellectual
aspirations, as well as high educational acquirements, displaced
superficial affectations."[10]

As we retrospectively view Arnold's intellectual development,
we see that "under his assumed conceit" he was finding ideas
of order that later became firm positions. He had outgrown the
easy epicureanism of Béranger; he did not return to the remote
spiritual latitudes of the *Bhagavad Gita;* and, although he paid
Obermann the tribute of a memorable poem in the fall of 1849,
the "unstrung will" and the "broken heart" are gradually replaced by other tones and other voices. The need for joy emerges.
It is difficult not to see injunctions to himself, as well as to
Clough, in the sequence of propositions that occur in one of his
letters. When courage is lost all is lost, he says—"muth verloren
alles verloren. In all religions the supreme Being is represented as
eternally rejoicing. . . . Deus est mortali juvare mortalem."[11] Reading Locke's *Essay Concerning Human Understanding* he finds

reason "the rock of refuge to this poor exaggerated surexcited humanity," and beyond Locke he finds in his new discovery of Spinoza a "positive and vivifying atmosphere."[12] Like Mycerinus, Lord Lansdowne's private secretary cultivated a private mental life of stoic withdrawal even among the "Barbarians" of Whig society; but, in addition, he was emerging from the refuge of Obermann's forests. He was quietly turning toward commitment, toward active engagement in the concerns of man in society.

Moreover, in London destiny had led him to the home of Sir William Wightman, a judge of the Queen's Bench. By July, 1850, Arnold, according to Clough, was "deep in a flirtation" with the judge's daughter.[13] The courtship had its small hazards. Tinker and Lowry print in *The Poetry of Matthew Arnold* a delightful letter from Arnold to Wyndham Slade reporting how he missed a meeting with Miss Wightman, a letter in which the mockery of Romantic style balances but does not cancel the sincerity of the sentiment.[14] The letter begins: "Last night for the 5th time the deities interposed: I was asked specially to meet the young lady—my wheels burned the pavement—I mounted the stairs like a wounded quaggha, the pulsations of my heart shook all Park Crescent—my eyes devoured every countenance in the room in a moment of time: she was at the opera, and could not come."

Clough described Frances Lucy Wightman as amiable and small, with fair complexion, aquiline nose, pleasing eyes—but "as a sort of natural enemy," for Arnold's engagement to her foreshadowed the end of Clough's breakfasting with Arnold twice a week, as they did in the early months of 1851.[15] To marry, Arnold needed a more assured future than that of secretary to an aging peer. Through the influence of Lord Lansdowne, he was appointed, on April 14, 1851, as one of Her Majesty's Inspectors of Schools. His mode of life promised to be nomadic and his income modest; but his future was secure. Almost at the outset of his career of thirty-five years, he could cheer his wife with a long hope of retiring to Italy on two hundred pounds a year.[16] Arnold was married on June 10, 1851, at Teddington, at the country house of Justice Wightman. Arnold told an Oxford friend, "You'll like my Lucy; she has all my sweetness and none of my airs."[17]

II *The Inspectorship*

In his *Autobiography* John Stuart Mill spoke of his era as one "in which education, and its improvement, are the subject of more, if not of profounder study than at any former period of English history. . . ."[18] Important changes in English elementary education began soon after the passage of the Great Reform Bill. In 1833 Parliament for the first time entered the field. In contrast to the tradition of Scotland ("Education is a passion in Scotland," said J. A. Froude), English schools were supported by fees, by private endowment, or by subscription.[19] In 1833 the House of Commons voted twenty-thousand pounds to aid in new school construction by the National Society for Church Schools or by the British and Foreign School Society. The former was Anglican, the latter non-denominational. Lord Russell set up a special committee of the Privy Council to administer the grant. The Lord President of the Privy Council was President of the Council on National Education.[20] In this capacity Lord Lansdowne served in 1834, again from 1835 to 1841, and finally from 1846 to 1852.

Dr. James Kay (later Sir James Kay-Shuttleworth) as secretary of the committee of the council established a system of inspectorships, apprentice-teachers, and additional financial incentives for teachers with a certificate from a training college. In 1846 Dr. Kay increased the number of inspectors to twenty, to visit about four thousand schools; and Arnold became part of this demanding and important system. When Parliament greatly increased its grant in aid, public opinion was widely fearful of the idea of a state system of education as implying state interference; and Arnold made it one of his tasks to combat this opinion. The state represented for him a force expressive of the best thought of a nation, a force making for order.

Under the system, Anglican clergymen inspected Anglican schools; Roman Catholics visited Roman Catholic schools that received state grants. Arnold, as a lay inspector, visited Dissenters' schools supported by the British and Foreign Schools Society. On one occasion he addressed Clough from Battersea: "I write to you from an evening sitting of the candidates for certificates at the Training School here. It is a Church of England place but such is my respectability, that I am admittted to their mysteries."[21] His work, however, was largely with the sizable dissenting group comprising the lower and middle class, the "Philistines" of his satirical and polemical prose. The term "Philistine," like the terms "Barbarian" or the "Populace," was, one must remember, a fictional abstraction for purposes of goading and persuading; in the reports that he rendered to his supervisor it is plain that Arnold was always humanely dealing with people. Education for him aimed to humanize and to civilize; its agents included not only books and physical conditions—space, light, air, but also the character of the teachers.

Arnold's duties as an inspector were great and fatiguing; his district was a large one. During his first fifteen months as inspector, for example, he was charged with one hundred and four schools in North and South Wales, and with some thirteen English shires.[22] "The irksomeness of my new duties," he once said, "was what I felt most, and during the first year or so this was sometimes almost insupportable. But I met daily in the schools with men and women discharging duties akin to mine, duties as irksome as mine, duties less well paid than mine, and I asked myself, Are they on Roses?"[23] Sometimes in the earlier years his wife accompanied him. One of his children, he recalled, was born in a lodging in Derby, "with a workhouse . . . behind and a penitentiary in front."[24] As the family increased, Mrs. Arnold remained in London.

His duties involved questioning the pupils ("if 5 cwt. of oatmeal cost 4..17..6, what do 126 cwt. cost?" "If 12 men can reap a field in 4 days, in what time can 32 men reap it?"); evaluating the teachers; and checking ventilation, drainage, book supplies, needlework in girls schools, and discipline.[25] If his letters record the burdens of his inspectorate, they also record his self-discipline and humor. "You are to come and see me," he wrote to his friend Wyndham Slade, "fighting the battle of life as an Inspector of Schools some day."[26] His published reports move toward the humanistic aim of education defined by Comenius whom he cited in his General Report for 1880: "to train generally all who are born men to all which is human."[27]

Arnold was never "Monsieur le Professeur Docteur Arnold, Directeur-Général de toutes les Écoles de la Grande Bretagne,"

[51]

as his "French friends" designated him; but he was recognized as a valuable public servant.[28] He was appointed a member of the important commission established in 1858 under the Duke of Newcastle to examine public education in Europe with a view to improving the English system. France, Switzerland, and Holland were assigned to him. Under the catch phrase "Payment by results," he attacked publicly, repeatedly, and with impunity the so-called "Revised Code" of 1862, which based allocation of grants on achievement tests of the pupils, a system supported by Lord Granville, by Robert Lowe, who was vice-president of the Committee of the Privy Council on Education, and by Robert R. W. Lingen, secretary of the committee.[29] Arnold played a part in the establishing of the Taunton Commission of 1864[30]; he travelled abroad again in 1865 as "Assistant Commissioner for Parts of the Continent of Europe" on Lord Lyttleton's Middle Class Schools Commission; and he was sent again in 1885 to Germany and France to look into their systems of free public education.

The reader of Arnold should remember that his production after 1851 as poet and critic both of literature and society was done in time wrested from a demanding professional career. The symbolic forests of Obermann and the pastoral haunts of the Scholar-Gipsy are countries of the mind. There were moments when he would have been willing to enter other positions—if the doors had not been closed. In 1856 he was dissuaded from going as a colonial secretary to Mauritius.[31] In 1863 he wrote his wife from Cambridge that he had made up his mind that he would "like the post of Master of Trinity."[32] In 1866 he sought a Charity Commissionership; in 1867 he applied unsuccessfully for the librarianship of the House of Commons; in 1869 Gladstone blocked his way to a Commissionership of Education—although in 1883 Gladstone, who abhorred Arnold's religious liberalism, awarded him a Civil List pension of two hundred and fifty pounds a year for his work in the field of letters.[33]

Even at the outset of his inspectorship Arnold made time for other incidental duties. Beginning in 1858, and continuing until the death of Judge Wightman in 1863, Arnold augmented his income by serving as a marshall to his father-in-law when he made his circuit. When his work as inspector was transferred to London, the circuit gratefully afforded him "a little country air and peace."[34] His duties included swearing in the grand jury and making abstracts of records—not to mention entertaining and being entertained. On one occasion Arnold wrote his mother concerning the Dean of Durham, who is said to have been "celebrated for gastronomy": "The Dean ought to have asked the Judge and all of us to dinner, but two judges lately kept him waiting for dinner till past nine o'clock, and he is said to have vowed he will never ask a judge again."[35]

III *Education Reports*

The unspecialized reader of Arnold's writings on education may recall the remark of G. B. Shaw about one of his own early novels: "He who reads *An Unsocial Socialist* will read anything." His voluminous prose in the area, in addition to Sir Francis Sandford's collection of his *Reports on Elementary Schools, 1852-1882*, runs to some six hundred and fifty pages in R. H. Super's definitive edition of the *Complete Prose Works of Matthew Arnold*. In terms of bulk *The Popular Education of France* (1861) and *Schools and Universities on the Continent* (1868) stand first; but in terms of literary interest the introduction to the former, which was subsequently published as the essay "Democracy" in *Mixed Essays* (1880) and *A French Eton; or, Middle Class Education and the State* (1864) are the most trenchant statements of his views on education; and they rise above the local, factual, informational character of the rest.[36]

On October 12, 1864, Arnold proposed that his publisher Alexander Macmillan include the introduction to *The Popular Education of France* as a part of *Essays in Criticism* (1865).[37] Had "Democracy" been included, it would not have been out of place, however specialized its origins; for its appeal is for objectivity, reasonableness, and greatness of spirit. In "Democracy" Arnold expresses attitudes that are elaborated in subsequent major works: for example, a sense of the dynamics of social change that can be directed to support generous human ideals; a liberal view of "culture" as integrating sophistication of mind and sophistication of conduct; an ideal of the state as embodying the best action of the nation; an optimism based on confidence in a morality that is beyond the flux of social change. It would be difficult to find in Arnold's work two complementary statements more expressive of his comprehensive humanism than these from "Democracy." The essence of *Culture and Anarchy* is latent in the first: "Culture without character is, no doubt, something frivolous, vain, and weak; but character without culture is, on the other hand, something raw, blind, and dangerous."[38] The essence of his reflections on theological subjects is latent in the second: "Human thought, which made all institutions, inevitably saps them, resting only in that which is absolute and eternal."[39]

A French Eton originally appeared as a series of three essays in *Macmillan's Magazine* in 1863 and 1864. Addressing a more general public than he did in *The Popular Education of France*, Arnold permitted himself the perilous luxury of his urbane irony. The introduction wonderfully alleges, and exposes, an indifference to the concerns of society on the part of the aristocracy, and on the part of the middle class an imperviousness to ideas and a preoccupation with economy:

To convey to Eton the knowledge that the wine of Champagne does not water the whole earth, and that there are incomes which fall below 5,000*l.* a year, would be an act of kindness towards a large class of British parents, full of proper pride, but not opulent. Let us hope that the courageous social reformer who has taken Eton in hand may, at least, reap this reward from his labours. Let us hope he may succeed in somewhat reducing the standard of expense at Eton, and let us prounounce over his offspring the prayer of Ajax:—"O boys, may you be cheaper-educated than your father, but in other respects like him; may you have the same loving care for the improvement of the British officer, the same terrible eye upon bullies and jobbers, the same charming gaiety in your frolics with the 'Old Dog Tray';—but may all these gifts be developed at a lesser price!"[40]

The interest today of the first two essays that comprise *A French Eton* is intermittent. The first seems to say that the French do better than the English, both in quality and in numbers, in giving state-supported education to the middle class. Although Arnold's plea for public education is important, the real interest attaches to his admiring account of Father

Lacordaire, a dedicated educator whose deliberate withdrawal from fame and whose serene inwardness were congenial characteristics to Arnold.

The second essay sends up a small display of satirical fireworks at the expense of conservative educational theories espoused by the London *Times*; this attack is followed by an account of certain privately operated middle-class schools with the aim of allaying middle-class fears about "state intervention." Arnold labored with the first two essays; about the third, he felt triumphant. "Read my Part III. in this *Macmillan*, and make Edward read it," he wrote to his mother April 29, 1864. "I have written, to my own mind, nothing better."[41] The third part with finer irony (Mr. Adderley, Mr. Baines, and Mr. Roebuck—those favorite Arnoldian whipping boys—are not spared) and subtler argumentation pleads for acceptance of the state as an appropriate agency in the civilizing activity of education. The Hebraism and the Hellenism of Arnold's own character are joined here. The appeal to intelligence is balanced by the appeal to morality: "God keeps tossing back to the human race its failures, and commanding it to try again."[42] The final ground of persuasion in this work is the essential ground of Arnold's work as a moralist—namely, that collective, social progress is only achieved by individual progress toward perfection of the spirit.

While *A French Eton* contains one of Arnold's best statements on democratic education, it also exhibits certain defects of sentiment. Perfection of the spirit is, although it may be the one thing needful, a most delicate subject to talk about. Even in the very moving Newmanesque appeal to the "Children of the Future" with which *A French Eton* concludes, we may be disturbed by amplification of "progress towards man's best perfection" as "the adorning and enobling of his spirit";[43] for "adorning" has overtones of self-consciousness, of a Pre-Raphaelite estheticism. And Arnold's terrible judgment on the United States in 1864 "transforming their spirit in the furnace of civil war" as a way toward refinement of temper in which "the lovers of perfection in America itself ought to rejoice" betrays on his part a capability for spiritual arrogance.[44] Inevitably Arnold's stance from time to time invited satirical barbs. For it is one thing for Dante's Pier delle Vigne to choose to withdraw into the refining fire; it is another for one of Her Majesty's Inspectors of Schools to express cosmic satisfaction in contemplating the disciplinary purgation of a civil war.

Such insensibility is not unique to *A French Eton,* even among the essays on education. In January, 1879, the Reverend F. Barham Zincke persuaded Arnold to address the Ipswich Working Men's College, of which he was principal. Arnold's address "Ecce, Convertimur ad Gentes," whose Latin title he translated and justified only in his final paragraph, made a plea for systematic state-supported public education at the secondary level. Arnold was pleased by his audience of six hundred persons and with its general response, although he heard "that some in the body of the room showed great signs of irritation at times."[45] He "refrained from all irony and playfulness" as unsuitable to a non-literary audience. Yet if the audience was at all cheered by an invitation to support middle-class education as a great democratic reform of the immediate future, we wonder what the impact of the final injunction was; for, without benefit of orientation to its setting in Dante, Arnold quoted: "Consider whereunto ye are born! Ye were not made to live like brutes, but to follow virtue and knowledge."[46] He began with Burke-like conciliatoriness; he ended, distressingly, not far from the tone of Coriolanus.

Arnold's demeanor in prose sometimes invited the barbs of his contemporaries, like W. H. Mallock, who satirized him as Mr. Rose in *The New Republic* (1877) and Frederic Harrison, who called him "the latest Apostle to the Gentiles." Nevertheless, even in Arnold's weakest essays he still has great force and eloquence in the area of his central concern—reason and conduct. *A French Eton* characteristically turns at the end to conduct and to the inward life. For Arnold was continuously and equally engaged by individual perfection and by the world of social practice.

But perhaps his own best formulation of the requirements of his age in the light of an increasing body of knowledge, increasing numbers to instruct, and increasing democracy in the governmental process comes at the close of his "General Report for the Year 1882." He borrowed the formulation from a sermon on charity schools that Bishop Joseph Butler had preached in 1745. Arnold deplored the exclusiveness of the upper classes in regarding education as their prerogative; he also insisted that democratic education train habits of mind, and not provide only inert facts. Commenting on the relevance of the sermon to the requirements of Victorian public education, Arnold wrote:

Every point is taken in it which most needs to be taken: the change in the world which makes "knowledges" of universal necessity now which were not so formerly, the hardship of exclusion from them, the absurdity and selfishness of those who are "so extremely apprehensive of the danger that poor persons will make a perverse use of even the least advantage, whilst they do not appear at all apprehensive of the like danger for themselves or their own children, in respect of riches or power, how much soever; though the danger of perverting these advantages is surely as great, and the perversion itself of much greater and worse consequences." But there is perhaps no sentence in the sermon which more deserves to be pondered by us than this: "Of education," says Butler, "*information itself is really the least part.*"[47]

The final sentence has, rhetorically, the weakness of a negative statement; but it directs the mind of the reader to the importance for Arnold of humanism as well as social humanitarianism.

CHAPTER 4

The Defense of Poetry

IN a frequently quoted letter to his mother, regarding the collected edition of his *Poems* in 1869, Arnold remarked,

My poems represent, on the whole, the main movement of mind of the last quarter of a century, and thus they will probably have their day as people become conscious to themselves of what that movement of mind is, and interested in the literary productions which reflect it. It might be fairly urged that I have less poetical sentiment than Tennyson, and less intellectual vigour and abundance than Browning; yet, because I have perhaps more of a fusion of the two than either of them, and have more regularly applied that fusion to the main line of modern development, I am likely enough to have my turn, as they have had theirs.[1]

The quarter century to which Arnold refers—1844 to 1869—covers the period of Arnold's entire poetic output, with the exception of those few late poems that live on in collected editions or in the most indulgently comprehensive anthologies. But the effortless survival of some two dozen poems that continue to engage the mind and the emotions of modern readers leaves no doubt about the solid basis of Arnold's hope that he would have his "turn." The distinctive temper that invests his poetry, granting all its flagrant failures of expression, and the body of ideas that the poems convey still speak directly to generations who discern in Arnold's compassionate voice an expression of man's existential situation in a world whose material origin is alien to the ideal aspirations that are the only mark of his humanity.

But it is not because Arnold's poetry conveys ideas that his poetry has validity, for some of the most "philosophic" writing (for example, Empedocles' discourse on the soul of man) most disastrously fails as poetic experience. His poetry has validity because, at its best (for example, in Callicles' song of "Cadmus and Harmonia," "The Forsaken Merman," "The Scholar-Gipsy," "Thyrsis," "Dover Beach," "Stanzas from the Grand Chartreuse"), Arnold's imaginatively created world gives us emotions and generates the ideas on which it invites us to reflect.

When Arnold thought that his poems represented "on the whole, the main movement of mind of the last quarter of a century," he was in a sense right. His poems do make us conscious of major intellectual turmoil of the age and of the longing for stability. We become aware of the changing concepts about man and nature, of the difficulty of achieving identity in a world of clamorously competing ideologies, of faith invaded by secularism, of fate and the individual will, and of turbulent historic and social change. Tennyson, the Brownings, Clough, Fitzgerald, the young Swinburne in their distinctive ways also confronted these issues.

In Arnold's narrative poems the topics are abstracted, however, from their local manifestations in scene or event. Empedocles, like the hero of Tennyson's *Maud*, possesses a Victorian sensibility; but, like Tennyson's Ulysses or Tithonus or Lucretius, he is detached from the contemporary scene. And, although one perceptive critic has pointed out unexpected Victorian references obtruding in the images of "Sohrab and Rustum," this poem is typical of Arnold's use of a remote myth to dramatize the fatality that limits action but that still leaves man scope to assert the dignity that gives him his humanity. Arnold's narrative poetry does not give a novelistic impression of the Victorian scene: He has no *Maud*, no *Amours de Voyage*, no *Christmas Eve and Easter Day*, no Bishop Blougram.

The "keepings" of his poetry, to use Gerard Manley Hopkins' term, are not conspicuously Victorian, although the habit of historical disguises itself is as Victorian as the social diversions of charades and the *bal costumé*, or the tableaux of Julia Margaret Cameron's photographs. We hear of iron times and confused alarms of struggle and flight, but we do not identify the cry of the children, or of the Irish, or of the Chartists; we do not identify the clangor of the Crimean War, or the Tübingen professors, or Geology and Astronomy, the "terrible Muses" that threatened Tennyson's Parnassus. Arnold's poetry creates the unsettled intellectual atmosphere of the age, but it seldom localizes its impressions in contemporary facts. On the other hand, the voice that speaks in the sonnets and lyrics is most frequently contemporary.

Apart from three or four exceptional poems in *New Poems* (1867), Arnold's best verse was published between 1849 and 1855. The two major volumes in the decade of the 1850's are *Empedocles on Etna, and Other Poems* (1852) by "A" and *Poems* (1853) with his own name on the title-page. Although *Poems* (1853) followed closely upon the *Empedocles on Etna,* it contained only nine new poems; and, with the exception of the long "Balder Dead" and one added lyric in the cycle "Faded Leaves," *Poems Second Series* (1855) was only a selection from earlier volumes. And the academic tragedy *Merope* (1858) is impressive mainly in its intention, not in its result.

In October, 1852, Arnold wrote Clough a letter expounding his poetic principles. The letter is full of import for his career as poet and as critic. The canons of English poetry, he said, are regrettably founded on the work of the Elizabethans, who are the major English poets. But modern poets—like Keats and Shelley, and he would include Tennyson—by pursuing the Elizabethan "exuberance of expression," "charm," "felicity," and "richness of images," are on the wrong track. They prefer parts to wholeness. They are on a wrong track because a mature age needs plainness of language, directness, severity; it needs wholeness in design, not "exquisite bits and images." "Modern poetry," he said "can only subsist by its *contents*: by becoming a complete *magister vitae* as the poetry of the ancients did: by including, as theirs did, religion with poetry, instead of existing as poetry only, and leaving religious wants to be supplied by the Christian religion, as a power existing independent of the poetical power."[2] The importance of subject matter, the connection between poetry and conduct, the ideal of an integrated sensibility, the interrelations of poetry and religion—these are repeatedly stressed in many ways throughout Arnold's poetry and prose. The first formal critical statement of them is in the important Preface to *Poems* (1853).

"I am fragments," Arnold told his sister "K" in 1849; and his poems too, he said, are fragments which cannot be made to accord.[3] The modern reader does not deplore their not being comprehensively the *magister vitae*, the guide of life, that Arnold believed modern poetry like Homer's poetry, ought to be. He regrets more the frequent Victorian didacticism; the jejune exclamations that stand for emotion; the thinness of language that is meant for severity; the vapid literalness of phrasing like "German Weimar," "Greece, Rome, England, France," and "the Carthusians' world-fam'd home"; or the failures of metaphysical imagery in the weakest manner of George Herbert:

> Long, long since, undower'd yet, our spirit
> Roam'd, ere birth, the treasuries of God;
> Saw gifts, the powers it might inherit,
> Ask'd an outfit for its earthly road.
>
> ("Self-Deception")
>
> Before man parted for this earthly strand,
> While yet upon the verge of heaven he stood,
> God put a heap of letters in his hand,
> And bade him make with them what word
> he could.
>
> ("Revolutions")

But Arnold survives the easy exposure of his poetical blunders. The poems that lack solution, if this is an element in what Arnold meant by "fragments," are just the poems that seem to modern readers to be successes. They seem best to realize Arnold's own ideas about "shaping," and to survive by their valid symbolism whereas his gnomic statements in verse give support to Sir Harold Nicolson's proposition that "the Victorians cared mainly for applied poetry."

I *Empedocles on Etna, and Other Poems*

Empedocles on Etna by "A" was published in October, 1852. Like the first volume by "A", it has its own thematic coherence. Stoicism in the face of chance and change, the relation between man and nature, the poet and the age he lives in, love, the ethical conscience and the inner life are prominently recurrent themes.

"Stanzas in Memory of the Author of 'Obermann'" explores with new intensity the sense of human isolation, the melancholy, and the nostalgia expressed in earlier poems like the "Memorial Verses," which he reprinted here. "Tristram and Iseult" deals with passion and fatality with greater complexity than did "The Forsaken Merman." The title poem "Empedocles on Etna" subsumes most of the major themes of the volume in an impressive and sustained work of lively intellectual interest, despite the poetic limitations of some parts. There are also other essential poems, like "Lines Written in Kensington Gardens," "Switzerland," and "A Summer Night."

"Stanzas in Memory of the Author of 'Obermann'" was composed in 1849. Obermann was the melancholy hero of Étienne Senancour's epistolary novel, to which both George Sand and Charles Sainte-Beuve appear to have directed the young Arnold's enthusiastic attention. Arnold's response was immediate and deeply personal; he admired the novel for its "profound inwardness" and "austere sincerity," and in November, 1848, he had himself discovered in the solitude of the Alpine pastures evoked by Obermann's meditative letters a mental refuge from the anxieties of his times. But it was a "refuge" for only an instant of poetic belief, for Arnold admits the impossibility of escape from oneself or one's age. The poignancy of this admission inspires his poetry, and his personal recognition of it impelled him to another than a poetic career.

The "Stanzas" is an elegy for Senancour in the guise of Obermann, but it is equally an elegy for mid-nineteenth-century man. In 1848 Arnold told Clough, ". . . since the Baconian era wisdom is not found in desarts."[4] This was his own long-standing perception, but he also believed that, since the Baconian era and especially in his own time, it had been more difficult to achieve the emotional detachment from the excitement and bewilderment of change that is necessary to pursue wisdom. Obermann, like Empedocles and the Scholar-Gipsy and indeed Iseult of Brittany, is a symbol of the integrity necessary for the quest. Yet his resignation, like that of Empedocles, is to a despair so penetrating that it precludes the endurance to pursue the quest.

In a tempestuous autumnal Alpine setting, the persona who meditates the poem is suffused with emotion recollected in agitation. He recalls the power of Obermann's letters to evoke the feel and sound of the Alps, their glaciers, pale crocuses, and pasturing kine:

> Yet, through the hum of torrent lone,
> And brooding mountain-bee,
> There sobs I know not what ground-tone
> Of human agony.

Subdued by this awareness, the poetic speaker reflects that there are three modes by which modern man has significantly confronted experience: those of Wordsworth, Goethe, and Obermann.

> But Wordsworth's eyes avert their ken
> From half of human fate;
> And Goethe's course few sons of men
> May seek to emulate.

Moreover, Goethe's calm is ascribed to his having passed his youth in the imagined tranquility of a more assured society.

> But we, brought forth and reared in hours
> Of change, alarm, surprise—
> What shelter to grow ripe is ours?
> What leisure to grow wise?
>
> Like children bathing on the shore,
> Buried a wave beneath,
> The second wave succeeds, before
> We have had time to breathe.
>
> Too fast we live, too much are tried,
> Too harass'd, to attain
> Wordsworth's sweet calm, or Goethe's wide
> And luminous view to gain.

What appears then to be left for the man of 1849 is a stoic demeanor, dramatized by Obermann's retreat into an Alpine hermitage where he is a kind of Byronic scholar-gipsy.

> How often, where the slopes are green
> On Jaman, has thou sate

By some high chalet-door, and seen
The summer-day grow late;

And darkness steal o'er the wet grass
With the pale crocus starr'd
And reach that glimmering sheet of glass
Beneath the piny sward,

Lake Leman's waters, far below!

But solitude is invaded by the special dilemma of the poet; and, echoing Faust's cry *"Zwei Seelen wohnen, ach! in meiner Brust,"* he cries,

Ah! two desires toss about
The poet's feverish blood.
One drives him to the world without,
And one to solitude.

Obermann can only enjoin renunciation. Arnold endows Obermann with Romantic symptoms, a "broken heart" and an "unstrung will." Nevertheless, by his recognition in all human experience of "the eternal note of sadness," as it is later called in "'Dover Beach," Obermann expresses a type of modern sensibility—by that and by his negative stoicism that echoes Achilles's words: *"Greater by far than thou are dead;/ Strive not! die also thou!"*

Within the context of the poem, the force of Obermann as a symbol for a way of life in Arnold's "damned times" is vitiated by the Wertherlike laceration of feeling and the "unstrung will." The stoicism is less persuasive than in the earlier "Resignation" in which the antithesis is between the active life and the contemplative; in the "Stanzas in Memory of the Author of 'Obermann,'" it is between the active life ("the world without") and the life of romantic feeling. Perhaps it was the despair in Obermann that led Arnold to exclude it as well as "Empedocles" from his *Poems* (1853).

A subdued but less Byronic stoicism pervades the "Memorial Verses. April, 1850." This elegy, written at the request of Edward Quillinan, Wordsworth's son-in-law and the friend of the Arnolds at Fox How, was reprinted in the "Empedocles" volume from

The Defense of Poetry

Fraser's Magazine (June, 1850). The subject of the poem is, as in W. H. Auden's "In Memory of W. B. Yeats," the death of a poet at a particular moment in history. The meaningfulness of the deaths of the poets regretted in "Memorial Verses" in part relates to the poets' modernity—to their having in some way shared "a wintry clime"—"this iron time/ Of doubts, disputes, distractions, fears." In this poem the triad Wordsworth, Goethe, and Obermann of the "Stanzas" becomes Byron, Goethe, and Wordsworth. The gain is not in the substitution, but in the greater balance and detachment with which the figures are treated.

In the "Stanzas in Memory of the Author of 'Obermann'" we are in effect asked to follow in the way of that "sad guide"; in "Memorial Verses" we are asked only to contemplate three symbolic figures, to appreciate their distinctive responses to man's fate. Byron represents passionate feeling in rebellion against necessity, Titanic through its grandeur, but not Promethean, for insight is not achieved, although something is gained through endurance. Goethe's insight is won through detachment and universal humanistic knowledge: "He said, *The end is everywhere,/ Art still has truth, take refuge there!*" Wordsworth expresses a sensibility kept freshly responsive to the joys of earth.

The Wordsworth of this poem is successfully disengaged from the elderly friend of the Arnolds at Fox How, and he is divested of his transcendental or his Christian religious feeling. Indeed, he is more like Arnold's own Callicles than a particular poet called Wordsworth. This is why we credit his assimilation into a Vergilian underworld, so un-Wordsworthian, so forlornly Arcadian:

> Ah, pale ghosts, rejoice!
> For never has such soothing voice
> Been to your shadowy world convey'd,
> Since erst, at morn, some wandering shade
> Heard the clear song of Orpheus come
> Through Hades, and the mournful gloom.

In one of his letters to Clough in 1849 Arnold objected, as "fatal to the sensuousness of poetry," to the "trying to go into and to the bottom of an object instead of grouping *objects*."[5] What Arnold has accomplished in grouping expresses in a rough way one of the successes of "Memorial Verses"; another one is that we are induced to forget the historical Byron, Goethe, and Wordsworth, so that we read it as a poem, not as versified literary criticism. This poem itself exemplifies very well what Arnold meant when he wrote to his mother that "a man is a just and fruitful object of contemplation much more by virtue of what spirit he is of than by virtue of what system of doctrine he elaborates."[6]

The confrontation of man with external nature, which is subordinate in "Memorial Verses," is a dominant theme of several other poems in the 1852 volume: "Self-Dependence," "Morality," "The Youth of Nature," "The Youth of Man," "A Summer Night," "Lines Written in Kensington Gardens." Some of these elaborate in more lyrical form the unbridgeable dichotomy between man and nature, or man and his reading of nature, expressed in "Quiet Work" in Arnold's first volume. Some readers have discovered particularly in "Lines Written in Kensington Gardens" a quality that elicits the term "Wordsworthian." The "Lines" evoke in the heart of London the illusion of a subdued pastoral setting:

> In this lone, open glade I lie,
> Screen'd by deep boughs on either hand;
> And at its end, to stay the eye,
> Those black-crown'd, red-boled pine-trees stand!
>
> Birds here make song, each bird has his,
> Across the girdling city's hum.
> How green under the boughs it is!
> How thick the tremulous sheep-cries come!
> . . . .
>
> Here at my feet what wonders pass,
> What endless, active life is here!
> What blowing daisies, fragrant grass!
> An air-stirr'd forest, fresh and clear.
>
> Scarce fresher is the mountain-sod
> Where the tired angler lies, stretch'd out,

> And, eased of basket and of rod,
> Counts his day's spoil, the spotted trout.

The mountain-sod is fresher; the songs of birds encounter city noises; the urban world "roars hard by." Yet the poet can find in the city the continuity of nature, an imagined happiness arising from fruition:

> Yet here is peace for ever new!
> When I who watch them am away,
> Still all things in this glade go through
> The changes of their quiet day.

But what the poet derives from his contemplation is at most only remotely Wordsworthian, for there is no enhanced sense of participation in the life of nature. There is nothing "far more deeply interfused"; there is no pleasure shared with "blowing daisies, fragrant grass." Instead, there is an apprehension of the incessant, naturalistic activity in process. And there is a final prayer, to a Plotinian "soul of all things," for inner peace, not for participation, and for stoicism to endure, for increased sympathy, not with objects in nature, but with men. To possess these qualities—peace, stoicism, human sympathy—is the meaning of "to live" in the final lines: "Calm, calm me more! nor let me die/ Before I have begun to live." Nature remains, as for Arnold typically it is, an emblematic pattern, whereas Wordsworth found in nature a religious experience. If Arnold detected religious experience anywhere, it was in the imaginative constructs of man.[7]

In "A Summer Night," which develops again this view of nature, the speaker—as in "Stanzas in Memory of the Author of 'Obermann'" and in "Lines Written in Kensington Gardens"—is a solitary quester, the *promeneur solitaire* of much Romantic art and poetry. In "A Summer Night" he wanders in a town where "the deserted moon-blanched street" and the "Silent and white, unopening" windows become symbols of the coldly repellent world. A sudden appearance of the moon itself fills the wanderer with emotion, recalling another and more tender moonlight scene—"But the same pacings to and fro,/ And the same vainly throbbing heart was there,/ And the same bright, calm moon."

To this solitary observer the moon suggests to man a third way of life between that of dispiriting convention and a rebellious Byronic individualism, a way embodying constancy, tranquillity, clarity.

These gifts, if they can be won, are won in some poems, such as "Self-Dependence" and "The Second-Best," by the discovery of selfhood and an inner life of obscure origin. The nature and origin of the personality and of the conscience interested Arnold, in relation both to the individual and to a continuing, but developing, ethical consciousness in society. The sonnet "Written in Butler's Sermons" in *The Strayed Reveller, and Other Poems* expresses impatience with eighteenth-century rationalistic analysis of personality into categories of "Affections, Instincts, Principles, and Powers,/ Impulse and Reason, Freedom and Control." Many of Arnold's other poems, in this and later volumes, touch the subject—but do not explore it—with symbols like "the fire within," "the central stream," "a single continent," "the sister-islands . . . Linking their coral arms under the sea," the Palladium. Orthodox terminology was unsuitable in Arnold's verse and prose to convey his sense of a shadowy but environing ethical force.

On March 3, 1865, Arnold wrote to his mother: "No one has a stronger and more abiding sense than I have of the 'daemonic' element—as Goethe called it—which underlies and encompasses our life; but I think, as Goethe thought, that the right thing is, while conscious of this element, and of all that there is inexplicable around one, to keep pushing on one's posts into the darkness, and to establish no post that is not perfectly in light and firm."[8] Arnold appears never to have found language by which to express very satisfactorily the daemonic element, which seems to operate in outward events and in inner feelings. Fate and destiny, "stream of tendency," *Zeitgeist*, and "the something not ourselves" are for Arnold various and tentative modes by which to express its multifarious operations.

Sometimes Arnold's statements about the inner life, as in "The Second-Best" and "Self-Dependence," are rather bleakly didactic. In "The Buried Life," on the other hand, with its anticipations of "Dover Beach," he writes with the eloquence that made "The Forsaken Merman" persuasive. The acquisition of insight and a sense of direction are achieved in "The Buried

Life" through a moment of tenderness. In satiric lines Arnold proposes,

> Fate, which foresaw
> How frivolous a baby man would be—
> By what distractions he would be possess'd,
> How he would pour himself in every strife,
> And well-nigh change his own identity—
> That it might keep from his capricious play
> His genuine self, and force him to obey
> Even in his own despite his being's law,
> Bade through the deep recesses of our breast
> The unregarded river of our life
> Pursue with indiscernible flow its way.

But in rare moments, "When a beloved hand is laid in ours," when there is profound mutual sympathy, "The eye sinks inward, and the heart lies plain,/ And what we mean, we say, and what we would, we know."

The lovers in Arnold's poetry seldom attain this union of feeling. The two sequences of poems that make up "Switzerland" and "Faded Leaves" deal with the theme of love; and, among them, the best in the 1852 volume, "To Marguerite, In Returning a Volume of the Letters of Ortis," poignantly regrets the isolation of the individual:

> Who renders vain their deep desire?—
> A God, a God their severance ruled!
> And bade betwixt their shores to be
> The unplumb'd, salt, estranging sea.

The title "Switzerland" was first assigned in *Poems* (1853) to an arrangement of poems of which six had appeared individually in the 1852 volume; and four other poems of 1852, together with a new poem, were arranged as "Faded Leaves" in *Poems. Second Series* (1855). Bibliographical and biographical details concerning them are lucidly and illuminatingly set forth in *The Poetry of Matthew Arnold: A Commentary*. The authors leave little doubt that "Faded Leaves" is associated with Arnold's courtship of Frances Lucy Wightman, just as "Switzerland" is with the earlier romantic Marguerite episode. Both of these sequences of lyrics recall in their form the nineteenth-century popularity of song-cycles like Beethoven's *An die Ferne Geliebte* and Schubert's *Die Winterreise* and *Die Schöne Müllerin*. They exist to express modes of feeling, and the narrative element in them is consequential only to hint a plausible circumstance to sustain and develop the mood. Unfortunately for Arnold's reputation in a circle wider than an academic one, they had no Beethoven or Schubert to support them.[9]

Arnold's most ambitious poem dealing with love is his impressive but uneven "Tristram and Iseult." Although it antedates the other celebrated nineteenth-century treatments of the story—Wagner's (1865), Tennyson's (1872), and Swinburne's (1882) —its claim to interest does not depend only upon its seniority. Yet few readers will share Arnold's own judgment that he "managed the story better than Wagner." Years later, after staying through the second act at a performance of *Tristan und Isolde* in Munich on March 2, 1886, Arnold, who was notoriously unmusical, wrote to his wife: "The second act is interminable, and without any action. The hero and heroine sit on a sofa and sing to one another about light and darkness, and their connexion with love."[10]

Arnold chose to tell his story, with which he confessed some dissatisfaction, partly in dramatic and partly in narrative form.[11] The narrative sections are spoken in the first person by a Tiresias-like commentator, who compassionately comprehends actions and emotions. The story itself, Arnold told Clough, was derived principally from two articles by Théodore de La Villemarqué on "Les poèmes gallois et les romans de la Table Ronde" in the *Revue de Paris* (1841).[12] The action, whose absence Arnold regretted in Wagner's opera, is only suggested in the three tableaux of his narrative: the dying Tristram, as he recalls in delirium his infatuation for Iseult of Ireland; the final meeting of the lovers; and the sadly compassionate Iseult of Brittany as she tells her children by Tristram another story of the fatality of love.

The fragments that comprise the action are comprehended and unified by a sensibility that sees all and feels all, but neither judges nor condemns. Most readers find adequate Tristram's delirious recollections of the obsessive image of the Irish Iseult;

most readers are uneasy with the brief declarations of the impassioned lovers. Yet the transformation of mutable human passion into the immutable tranquillity of death or art, symbolized by the tapestry at the close of Part II, and the tonal achievement of Part III, through which the widowed Iseult of Brittany becomes heroic in her quiet fortitude, are memorable expressions of Arnold's power to write "poetry of experience."

Like "The Forsaken Merman," this poem dramatizes the unconstrainable nature of love. Iseult of Brittany expresses through her comprehending acquiescence not apathy, nor the icy despair of Obermann, but active love. Arnold's liking for "Tristram and Iseult," which he reprinted in the successive collected editions of his poems, is understandable; for it avoids the "thinking aloud" in poetry that he deplored; it gains its effectiveness by its "grouping" of objects; and, while it may not "animate," as he thought "The Scholar-Gipsy" failed to do, it ends with the fair Iseult's quiet and humanistic triumph over event. Arnold's treatment of love has much that reminds one of Anton Chekhov's Naturalism —of his compassionate yet ironic sense of the isolation of the individual, the compulsion of emotional experience, the limits of accident and will that circumscribe human happiness, and the quality of happiness that remains available to man.

Clough, who had left England in 1852 for Cambridge, Massachusetts, reviewed *Empedocles on Etna* in the *North American Review* (July, 1853). He was puzzled to understand "Tristram and Iseult," whose ending he thought "a sort of faint musical mumble." He was even more depreciatory of the title poem of the volume with its "pseudo Greek inflation of the philosopher musing above the crater, and the boy Callicles singing myths upon the mountain." It was Clough as well as his own fictional hero Claude who in *Amours de Voyage* cried, "Utter, O some one, the word that shall reconcile Ancient and Modern!"; but Clough never thought that Arnold accomplished this union. Perhaps Clough shared about "Empedocles" the reservations of their Oxford friend John Campbell Shairp. Shairp wrote to Clough concerning Arnold from Dresden on July 24, 1849:

He was working at an 'Empedocles'—which seemed to be not much about the man who leapt in the crater—but his name & outward circumstances are used for the drapery of his own thoughts. I wish Matt w^d give up that old Greek form but he says he despises all the modern ways of going about the art & will stick to his own one. Also I do not believe in nor feel with that great background of fatalism or call it what you will which is behind all his thought. But he thinks he sees his way.[13]

Many modern readers will themselves feel a tempered admiration for this dramatic poem as a whole, at least for its ineptness as drama, however much they may respond to Callicles' songs as individual poems or find absorbing Empedocles' central monologue as reflecting the dilemma of a Victorian intellectual.

Arnold's drama presents an Empedocles estranged from his age; he is impatient of human folly, burdened by his own solitude; and his escape is to plunge into the crater of Mt. Etna. Although he is a physician, poet, and philosopher, Empedocles' span of knowledge brings him despair, not the Olympian calm that Arnold attributed to the universally minded Goethe. Arnold discerned an analogy between Victorian England and Sicily in the fifth century B.C.; he saw parallels in the alienation of man from his universe, in the confusion of rapid change that precludes the leisure congenial for intellectual ripening, in the general corruption invading society—"Tyranny, pride and lust fill Sicily's abodes." His description of the situation of Empedocles in the 1853 Preface recalls his outcries to Clough against his own age— "the height to which knowledge is come, the spread of luxury, our physical enervation, the absence of great natures. . . .";[14] he spoke of Empedocles as "having survived his fellows, living on into a time when the habits of Greek thought and feeling had begun fast to change, character to dwindle, the influence of the Sophists to prevail."[15]

Among the Arnold manuscripts in the Yale University Library there is a page outlining, as Tinker and Lowry phrase it, "the poem he wanted to create." The discrepancy between the finished *Empedocles* and what the design suggests may be part of Arnold's analysis of its failure, beyond his analysis of its failure in his 1853 Preface. In the Yale manuscript Arnold wrote of Empedocles:

> He sees things as they are—the world as it is—God as he is: in their stern simplicity.
> The sight is a severe and mind-tasking one: to know the mysteries which are communicated to others by fragments, in parables.[16]

Empedocles in the poem does not share this vision with the reader. Things as they are and the world as it is, if this includes the human world, do not reveal a "stern simplicity." For Empedocles there are no Gods, for the Gods are but human inventions upon which man vents his rage and excuses his own partial vision. In the human world there are only confusion, frustration, and folly. The power of sympathy between man and nature diminishes with lived experience. Empedocles tells us that he once enjoyed "the delightful commerce of the world," but now he is "dead to every natural joy," he "has no minute's breathing space allow'd/ To nurse his dwindling faculty of joy." Arnold has, unfortunately, found no poetic symbol to convey the intellectual awakening by which Empedocles saw "things as they are." A similar inadequacy severely weakens Tennyson's persuasiveness at the climatic moment of *In Memoriam* when in Poem 95 the mourner claims to apprehend "that which is." It is a strength of the later myth of Arnold's questing Scholar-Gipsy that he awaits "the spark from heaven"; for, as in Browning's "Childe Roland to the Dark Tower Came," the human triumph is in the questing, not in the event. Empedocles is alleged to have rejoiced in the search and in the discovery, but he discovers to the reader mainly his recollected emotions and present despair.

On the other hand, Callicles, the young harp player whose songs are intended, however ironic their result, to alleviate Empedocles' depression, expresses his conceptions through myths that are viable. Arnold rescued them from the drama and reprinted them later as independent lyrics: "The Lost Glen," "Cadmus and Harmonia," "Typho," "Marsyas," and "Apollo" or "Apollo Musagetes." They have their dramatic fitness in *Empedocles*, and they have their own integrity. In his Arcadian sylvan world Chiron, "the aged Centaur" who instructs Achilles, is the archetypal poet, both Hesiodic and Homeric. The struggling rebel Typho, pinned under the weight of Etna, lies victim to the sheer power of an unyielding and disdainful Jove. Shielding his eyes from Apollo's scornful flaying of Marsyas, the young Olympus expresses the terror of man before the intolerable severity of what he must endure. Cadmus and Harmonia, transformed into "bright and aged snakes" in a moment of divine mercy, live in serene placidity in the cool and buoyant pastoral world that Arnold's language has made for them. Like Raphael in Goethe's Prologue in Heaven, Callicles' final song gladly celebrates a revelation that Empedocles never won: the endless renewal and continuity and creativity in things.

II Poems (1853)

Very soon after the publication of *Empedocles on Etna* Arnold projected a third volume of poetry. By May, 1853, he had completed his epyllion "Sohrab and Rustum," "by far the best thing I have yet done."[17] He was greatly encouraged to have heard the report that Lord John Russell had said, "In his opinion Matthew Arnold was the one rising young poet of the present day."[18] In August, "nearly stupified by 8 months inspecting," he wrote to Clough from Fox How that he was planning a general preface for the new volume.[19] The Preface was completed by October 10. ". . . there is a certain *Geist* in it I think," he told Clough, "but it is far less *precise* than I had intended. How difficult it is to write prose: and why? because of the *articulation of the discourse*: one leaps over these in Poetry—places one thought cheek by jowl with another without introducing them—but in prose this will not do."[20]

In *Poems*, published in November, "Sohrab and Rustum," "The Scholar-Gipsy," "Requiescat," and "Philomela" were among the new poems. "Empedocles on Etna" was excluded. The Preface elaborated the reasons in Arnold's first and one of his most important critical essays. The Preface is at once his manifesto and his defense of poetry.

Arnold begins by justifying his choice of the subject of Empedocles on the basis of its essential modernity, for in the last years of the life of Empedocles "the calm, the cheerfulness, the disinterested objectivity [of early Greek genius] have disappeared: the dialogue of the mind with itself has commenced;

modern problems have presented themselves; we hear already the doubts, we witness the discouragement, of Hamlet and of Faust."[21] But he has now excluded the poem because it fails in what, on the high authority of Hesiod and of Schiller, is an end of art: to inspirit and rejoice, to "convey a charm, and infuse delight." This aim is not accomplished by a portrayal of "a continuous state of mental distress," by a situation in which the suffering finds no vent in action. "'All art,' says Schiller, 'is dedicated to Joy.'"

What Arnold has proposed to justify his decision becomes conspicuously an important part of his total endeavor: "to establish Joy," as Lionel Trilling says.[22] The indifference of the *Bhagavad Gita* and the icy despair of an Obermann do not have the power to stay. For Arnold joy is a message not only of Hesiod and Schiller but also of George Sand and Wordsworth. He comes to see it as a message of the Bible: "'Rejoice and give thanks!' exhorts the Old Testament; 'Rejoice evermore!' exhorts the New."[23] Proverbs is "a delicious book."[24] Even in the melancholy *Obermann* Arnold found an injunction that he repeatedly entered in his own meditative Note-Books: "The aim for man is to augment the feeling of joy, to make our expansive energy bear fruit, and to combat, in all thinking beings, the principle of degradation and misery."[25] What Arnold did not say in his Preface, for it would have been irrelevant even if we could know he had foreseen it, is how important to his future career was the ethical and metaphysical ground on which he chose to suppress *Empedocles.*

Another point of departure for the Preface is the need that Arnold felt to reply to his critics. R. S. Rintoul, the editor of *The Spectator,* had publicly declared: "The Poet who would really fix the public attention must leave the exhausted past, and draw his subjects from matters of present import, and *therefore* both of interest and novelty."[26] Arnold represents this generalization as typical of a tendency in current criticism and therefore as a sufficient occasion for asking, with neo-Classic confidence in the principle of universality, "What are the eternal objects of poetry, among all nations, and at all times?" The simple seeming answer is human actions. The real answer is "excellent" human actions, which Arnold defines, with echoes of Wordsworth's Preface to *Lyrical Ballads* (1802), as those that appeal most powerfully "to the great primary human affections: to those elementary feelings which subsist permanently in the race, and which are independent of time."[27] For Arnold these feelings are not exemplified by Wordsworth's Solitary or Byron's Harold, or Goethe's Hermann and Dorothea; but they are exemplified by Achilles, Oedipus, and Dido. The works of the ancients, expressed in the theory of Aristotle and in the practice of their poets, proclaim to us: "All depends upon the subject; choose a fitting action, penetrate yourself with the feeling of its situations; this done, everything else will follow."[28]

In fact, even in the Preface Arnold perceives that all does not depend on the subject, "the red herring of Victorian criticism" in F. W. Bateson's phrase.[29] Much depends on what Goethe called *Architectonicé*, on proportion, grouping, form, not on the accessories, the beautiful parts, the "felicitous words and images" that make Shakespeare so dangerous a model for modern poets— as witness the interesting failures of John Keats. It is the simplicity of expression and the subordination of detail to the whole that contribute to the *grand style* of which the ancients are the masters.

For Arnold there is a special relevance in all this for his own age. For in a time of confused aims, "wanting in moral grandeur," "an age of spiritual discomfort," a time offering to the artist a bewildering variety of attractive models, one needs a guide to counsel discipline, to save the talent of the future at least from the penalties that arise from caprice. Arnold modestly yet firmly sets himself in this Preface the dual but coordinated role that harmonizes his multiple activities: fortified by Aristotle and the ancient poets, he aims to elucidate the grand moral effects of style; fortified by Goethe and the statesman-historian B. G. Neibuhr, he intends to direct his own way and that of others through what is "impeding and disabling" in the Victorian age.

Poetry might provide a *magister vitae*, but Arnold was committing himself to a task which he could only accomplish, if it could be accomplished, through prose discourse. It is difficult not to believe that Arnold was to some degree conscious of his commitment. For in June, 1852, when he was thinking about the Preface, he expressed regret that "hitherto the gifted have astonished and delighted the world, but not trained or inspired or in any real way changed it." "I am sure however," he concluded, "that in the air of the present time il nous manque d'aliment, and that we deteriorate in spite of our struggles—like a gifted Roman falling on the uninvigorating atmosphere of the decline of the Empire. Still nothing can absolve us from the duty of doing all we can to keep alive our courage and activity."[30]

By the ethical standards of the Preface, Arnold thought that even "The Scholar-Gipsy" failed; for it awakened only "a pleasing melancholy."[31] What men needed was "something to *animate* and *enoble* them." That "Sohrab and Rustum," he thought, did. It was placed first in *Poems* (1853). Some modern critics have seen in the fatal conflict, in which the powerful father subdues his warrior son, an adumbration of a psychological conflict between Matthew Arnold and his father. It is difficult to see how this interpretation is generated from within the poem, or that it is useful in enhancing the reader's contemplation of what Arnold felt was a "noble action of a heroic time." As with the Forsaken Merman and Iseult of Brittany, we witness the confrontation of a human figure with an ironic human event. Arnold comes near to expressing in these poems what he so fruitlessly tried to express in his play *Merope—"a sentiment of sublime acquiescence in the course of fate, and in the dispensations of human life."*[32]

"Sohrab and Rustum" has the noble subject, the heroic characters, the preciseness and firmness that the 1853 Preface demand, and much of the plainness and directness of expression, which, in his lectures on Homer, Arnold included among the characteristics of Homeric style. The poem has the severely tragic circumstance that illustrates the "keynote to the Iliad," which Arnold liked to express by using Goethe's words: "From Homer and Polygnotus I every day learn more and more clearly that in our life here above ground we have, properly speaking, to enact Hell."[33] It has also enobling echoes of the King James version of the Old Testament, and of Miltonic epic similes. It also has the admirably moving close in which Sohrab is left alone with his grief, and with the body of his son, while habitual activity resumes in the opposing camps, and the majestic but inexorable life of things flows on—a life that is embodied in the final image of the river achieving its goal in waters "bright/

And tranquil, from whose floor the new-bathed stars/ Emerge, and shine upon the Aral Sea."

But to some readers the enobling echoes seem a little strained. They regret the lack of motivation, the lapses into the frigid Neoclassicism of lines like "Unwillingly the spirit fled away,/ Regretting the warm mansion which it left./ And youth, and bloom, and this delightful world"; or the Victorian anachronisms in superimposed decorative passages like this:

> —all down his cold white side
> The crimson torrent ran, dim now and soil'd,
> Like the soil'd tissue of white violets
> Left, freshly gather'd, on their native bank,
> By children whom their nurses call with haste
> Indoors from the sun's eye.

There is fine irony in the incidental comment of Tinker and Lowry that the reputation of "Sohrab and Rustum" has been "sustained—with the help of many schoolmasters." Some readers turn with greater pleasure to the Landorlike concision of "Requiescat," to the brief and poignant intensity of "Philomela," and to the creative mythmaking in "The Scholar-Gipsy."

Arnold prefaced "The Scholar-Gipsy" with an anecdote from Joseph Glanville's *The Vanity of Dogmatizing*. But the gipsy lore that Glanville's scholar looked for is mesmerism; Arnold's scholar begins with a similar quest, but by a sleight of words— "But it needs heaven-sent moments for this skill"—he induces the reader to believe that he pursues a philosophic insight, a knowledge of the nature of things and the joy in nature.

"The Scholar-Gipsy" is indebted to John Keats, whom Arnold once dismissed as an "inspired 'cheeper.' "[34] In transforming into a symbol the anecdote that he found, Arnold learned a lesson from the "Ode to a Nightingale" with its remarkable transformation of the concrete nightingale into an immortal one that acceptably unites the unchanging life of nature and the human capability for joy. The Scholar-Gipsy is assimilated into the seasonal life of nature and the habitual life of man in his rural setting, as he pursues with integrity his spiritual quest. More satisfying than the "soil'd tissue of white violets" is the plain exactness in this poem of "the frail-leaved, white anemones" or "purple orchises with spotted leaves," or the Keatsian sensuousness of "Dark bluebells drenched with dews of summer eves." If the compulsive cry "No, no, thou hast not felt the lapse of hours!/ For what wears out the life of mortal men?" has overtones of Keats's "Thou wast not born for death immortal bird,/ No hungry generations tread thee down," it is no less effective; and the poetic statement that it introduces of the bafflement of the age seems more poignant than the discursive monologue in "Empedocles on Etna." The fugitive light of self-discovery that The Scholar-Gipsy pursues has a greater possibility of being found than any that can come to Arnold's wan Obermann, "All shipwreck in thy own weak heart."

III   *Poems. Second Series*

Towards the end of 1854 Arnold sent his mother six copies, including one for Mrs. Wordsworth, of a new selection of his poems with the title *Poems. Second Series,* and dated 1855. The major poem in the volume—and, except for "Separation," the only new one—was "Balder Dead," which Arnold had finished at Fox How in September, 1854. As in the case of "Sohrab and Rustum," the title was originally followed by the words "An Episode" to heighten the sense of its being an epic fragment. Arnold hoped it would support the reputation "Sohrab and Rustum" had gained; and he preferred it, as did A. P. Stanley, to that poem. His treatment of the Norse story of Balder's death, burial, and descent to Hell is, as critics have noted, more Homeric and Vergilian than Icelandic. The "fire" that Arnold thought was an element of Icelandic poetry is subdued; and Balder, exiled from Asgard, emerges at the end as another Arnoldian seeker of a new and better world.

Like Wordsworth, Arnold wished to modify the sensibility of his generation, for in his way he deplored the presence of "gross and violent stimulants" that blunted human capabilities. His occupation as school inspector brought him into daily contact with the values and personalities of masses of people. His own poetic talent was for articulating modes of melancholy in the face of the human situation, for exhibiting symbolic figures assuming postures indicative of their comprehending response to human tragedy. This kind of poetry could not provide a *magister vitae*. The early exhaustion of Arnold's poetic talent seems to have been intimately related to the limited number of the themes he could express poetically. His was a talent sufficient to insure a firm reputation, but it was not sufficient to fulfill his much more versatile capabilities.

CHAPTER 5

"The Hideous Title of 'Professor'"

THE conscience of the Rugbeian, which Clough's fictional uncle in *Dipsychus* found much too tender in his nephew's generation, troubled Arnold. It is manifest in the poems and in the correspondence, where it sometimes expresses itself in a malaise: "How life rushes away, and youth. One has dawdled and scrupled and fiddle faddled—and it is all over"; "I am past thirty, and three parts iced over—and my pen, it seems to me is even stiffer and more cramped than my feeling"; "I seem to myself to have lost all ressort." It sometimes expresses itself in a clear opposition between drift and duty—"Still nothing can absolve us from the duty of doing all we can to keep alive our courage and activity."[1]

As late as March 31, 1856, Arnold was writing to his brother William, recently appointed director of public instruction in the Punjab, that he, like his brother, "felt the absurdity and disadvantage" of their hereditary connection "in the minds of all people with education." Yet his brother would throw himself heartily into his work, he said; "I on the contrary half cannot half will not throw myself into it, and feel the weight of it doubly in consequence. I am inclined to think it would have been the same with any active line of life on which I had found myself engaged—even with politics—so I am glad my sphere is a humble one and must try more and more to do something worth doing in my own way, since I cannot bring myself to do more than a halting sort of half-work in other people's way."[2] At the same time he recognized, as he wrote his brother, when commenting on a new volume of Ruskin's *Modern Painters,* that the one thing needful was not the perception of isolated verities, but of the ordering and interconnections of truth.

He wrote this letter from the Athenaeum, the London club to

which he had been elected in the preceding month, to his great pleasure. "The Athenaeum," he wrote to his sister "K," "is a place at which I enjoy something resembling beatitude."[3] The club gave him access to books, and its great drawing room gave him a place in which to write after the duties of school inspection were over; for Arnold's original circuit had changed and now included the eastern counties and a number of schools in London. Arnold soon found an activity in education where he could develop a style and voice of his own in a sphere less humble than that of district schools. And he found occasions for writing in whatever leisure his heavy, routine duties left him.

In the spring of 1857 Arnold enthusiastically engaged in the contest for the election of the Professor of Poetry at Oxford University. To win this contest would give him at once prestige, renewed association with the Oxford to which he was profoundly attached, and a forum for his sophisticated thought. We know that in April he wrote to at least two of his contemporaries at Oxford, the Reverend William Lucas and the Reverend George Henry Sumner, urging them to go down to the Oxford Convocation on May 5 to vote for him. His opponent, the Reverend John Ernest Bode, was actively supported by the Christ Church men. Arnold's apprehensiveness about the result and his relieved delight in his final success are reflected in a letter to his mother:

Keble voted for me after all. He told the Coleridges he was so much pleased with my letter (to the electors) that he could not refrain. . . . I had support from all sides. Archdeacon Denison voted for me, also Sir John Yarde Buller, and Henley, of the high Tory party. It was an immense victory—some 200 more voted than have ever, it is said, voted in a Professorship election before. It was a great lesson to Christ Church, which was rather disposed to imagine it could carry everything by its great numbers.[4]

The Oxford professorship brought Arnold back to a scene with which he had already many associations, and which he continued to invest with the union of Romantic sentiment and spiritual feeling that colors "The Scholar Gipsy" and "Thyrsis," and glows in the famous close of the Preface to *Essays in Criticism* (1865):

[82]

Beautiful city! so venerable, so lovely, so unravaged by the fierce intellectual life of our century, so serene!

"There are our young barbarians, all at play!" And yet, steeped in sentiment as she lies, spreading her gardens to the moonlight, and whispering from her towers the last enchantments of the Middle Age, who will deny that Oxford, by her ineffable charm, keeps ever calling us nearer to the true goal of all of us, to the ideal, to perfection, to beauty, in a word, which is only truth seen from another side?[5]

The duties of the Professor of Poetry included the delivery in alternate years of the Creweian oration at the Oxford Commemoration, or Encaenia; and the delivery of three lectures on poetry each year. Until Arnold's incumbency the commencement oration in memory of the benefactors of Oxford and the lectures on poetry had been given in Latin; Arnold, with the permission of the authorities, gave his lectures on poetry in English. In 1862 he was honored by election for a second term of five years to the professorship. In 1877 he declined a proposal that he stand again for the office.[6]

During the years from 1857 to 1867, Arnold delivered Creweian orations in 1858, 1860, 1864, and 1866, at the traditionally and tumultuously noisy Commemoration exercises. "That absurd scene" was Arnold's phrase; *The Times* called the Encaenia "a sort of festival of misrule."[7] Texts of only the first and third of Arnold's Latin orations are extant. However, the lectures on poetry in English, which he gave with considerable irregularity, established Arnold as a literary critic. Most of them were published in magazines before they became books. Some comprise *On Translating Homer* and *On Translating Homer. Last Words* (1862); some found a place in the wide-ranging *Essays in Criticism* (1865); some make up *On the Study of Celtic Literature* (1867); others remained uncollected and survived their occasion in periodical publication; of yet others, there is only a fragmentary record.

I *"On the Modern Element in Literature"*

Arnold delivered his inaugural lecture "On the Modern Element in Literature" in the Sheldonian Theatre at Oxford on November 14, 1857.[8] This essay, which Arnold later dispraised as being in "a rather high-horse academic style,"[9] seems to us who read it retrospectively to develop from the Preface of 1853 and from comments in earlier letters to Clough, and to anticipate lines of thought central to Arnold's later critical prose.

He begins the lecture with the premise that the modern element or spirit in an age is discernible insofar as the age seeks and achieves knowledge of itself. Such knowledge he calls "an intellectual deliverance." It is revealed most often through the poetry of a nation; but it manifests itself especially in a critical spirit, in an "endeavour after a rational arrangement and appreciation of facts."[10] The Athens of Pericles exemplifies an epoch that characteristically had the ability to comprehend itself as it surveyed the multiplicity of facts that constitute the social and political spectacle of the times, and it was an epoch that had a literature commensurate with the complex image it had to express. Arnold reminds his audience that he had said of Sophocles that he "saw life steadily, and saw it whole." But Thucydides also, in a lucid style, treated a great and complex subject, the Peloponnesian War; but, if one turns to Sir Walter Ralegh's *History of the World,* one finds fantastic questions posed for inquiry and a fantastic style. By the ingenious art of Arnold's verbal play these observations demonstrate a conclusion that could not have surprised those familiar with the 1853 Preface: the modernity of fifth-century Athens; indeed, its greater relevance than the age of Elizabeth I.

To express the idea of the commensurateness of style with thought, Arnold chose the words *adequacy* and *adequate.* The poetry of Sophocles, for example, he says is remarkable for "its unrivalled *adequacy.*" The looseness of the term makes one think sympathetically of William James's just protest about another of Arnold's favored critical terms. "His ultimate heads of classification, too, are lamentable," James said; "Think of 'interesting' used as an absolute term!!"[11] *Adequacy,* Arnold goes on to explain, represents "human nature developed in a number of directions, politically, socially, religiously, morally developed— in its completest and most harmonious development in all these directions."[12] And the mark of the creative writer who has understood human nature in this way, who has mastered "the problem of human life" is, in Arnold's phrase, "serious cheerfulness."

Thus Lucretius and Vergil, living at a great and important epoch, lack *adequacy*; for they lack cheerfulness. Feelings of depression and ennui pervade them. And what of Horace? He is lacking in seriousness. One must then, recognizing the special wholeness of the achievement of "Greek litreature, and, above all, of Greek poetry," measure one's own intellectual history by its standards, which are absolute.

"On the Modern Element in Literature" echoes Arnold's reminder that one must begin with an idea about the world in order not to be prevailed over by the world's multitudinousness. His effort to view literature in the large perspective of history and his concern with epochs and "culminating" ages anticipate the perspectives of "The Function of Criticism at the Present Time" (1864), as does his aim to assist an intellectual deliverance. At the same time his description of the special adequacy of Sophocles—"the harmonious development" in many directions: political, social, religious, moral—connects the issues of intellect and morality, and anticipates the theme of *Culture and Anarchy*. Arnold's down-grading of Lucretius because of his tone of depression and ennui reminds us of his reservations about his own Empedocles and his Scholar-Gipsy, and his dismissal of Horace for want of seriousness connects this early critical essay with "The Study of Poetry" (1880), in which he expresses a similar view of Chaucer.

The 1853 Preface and "On the Modern Element in Literature" formulate his basic critical attitudes, and they also express his own role in his times. He believed that his age presented "a significant spectacle to contemplate," and that there existed "the desire to find the true point of view from which to contemplate this spectacle."[13] "He who has found that point of view, he who adequately comprehends this spectacle, has risen to the comprehension of his age: he who communicates that point of view to his age, he who interprets to it that spectacle, is one of his age's intellectual deliverers."[14] It is just a little ironic that a Professor of Poetry who in that official position declared that poetry most adequately interpreted an epoch, should have found in prose the versatile instrument for his work as critic, satirist, moralist, while his poetry, at its best, expresses the lassitude, the ennui, the alienation that are elements in the dialogue of the modern mind with itself.

Perhaps Arnold's awareness of the deficiency of his argument made him reluctant to publish this lecture for a dozen years. He had planned it to inaugurate not only his professorship, but a series of lectures on the subject; and he had hoped to publish them in book form.[15] The book never appeared. Arnold channeled his energies in other directions.

II *Merope*

Arnold was himself busy writing a tragic drama when he said in his inaugural lecture, ". . . the dramatic form exhibits, above all, *the actions of man as strictly determined by his thoughts and feelings; it exhibits, therefore, what may be always accessible, always intelligible, always interesting.*"[16] Among his early poems are his "Fragment of an 'Antigone'" and "Fragment of Chorus of a 'Dejaneira.'" He had long planned a major tragedy, which he never finished, on Lucretius, although he was actively reading for it or working on it in the years 1855 to 1858.[17] To judge from the view of Lucretius in "On the Modern Element in Literature," Arnold regarded him as a spirit akin to his own Obermann and as out of keeping with the temper of Sophocles whose tragedies he was studying again in 1857 ("And what a man! What works!"[18]) while he concurrently composed his tragedy, the academic *Merope*. The Oxford appointment added its impetus to the completion of this work by the fall of 1857.[19] It was published in December with an elaborate Preface, although the title page is dated 1858. *Merope*, he told Mme. Fanny Blackett du Quaire, "is calculated rather to inaugurate my Professorship with dignity than to move deeply the present race of *humans*."[20] There is a trace of disdain for the reading public in his remark, for Arnold thought of *Merope* as more than academic. He even seriously imagined it as a stage vehicle for Helena Faucit, to whom he wrote and with whom he discussed the remote possibility of a production.

Merope is the story of a mother who awaits the return of her son Aepytus, to avenge his father's murder by his step-father, Polyphontes. The myth had already been the subject in the eighteenth century of plays by Maffei, Voltaire, and Alfieri. Arnold's austere version will interest the Arnold scholar, but it attracts only those general readers who are as intrepid as they are curious.

The variable Time-Spirit, which breathes upon literary reputations, took a dreadful revenge upon Arnold's own facetiousness. In the age of Stracheyian biography and criticism, Hugh Kingsmill published a facetious study of Arnold; inevitably, he turned his attention upon Arnold's favorite child *Merope*. To exemplify Arnold's sense for dramatic incident he cited Merope's recognition of her sleeping son whom she supposes to be her son's alleged murderer:

MEROPE
A more just stroke than thou gav'st my son
Take——

MEROPE *advances towards the sleeping* AEPYTUS, *with the axe uplifted. At the same moment* ARCAS *reenters.*

ARCAS (*to the Chorus*)
Not with him to council did the King
Carry his messenger, but left him here.

Sees MEROPE *and* AEPYTUS.

O Gods! . . .

MEROPE
Foolish old man, thou spoil'st my blow!

ARCAS
What do I see? . . .

MEROPE
A murderer at death's door. Therefore no words!

ARCAS
A murderer? . . .

MEROPE
And a captive to the dear next-of-kin he murder'd. Stand, and let vengeance pass!

ARCAS
Hold, O Queen, hold! Thou know'st not whom thou strik'st . . .

MEROPE

I know his crime.

ARCAS

Unhappy one! thou strik'st—

MEROPE

A most just blow.

ARCAS

No, by the Gods, thou slay'st—

MEROPE

Stand off!

ARCAS

Thy son!

MEROPE

Ah! . . .

She lets the axe drop, and falls insensible.

To exemplify Arnold's feeling for the Greek tragic chorus, Kingsmill unkindly proposed this example of Arnold's verse:

> But the signal example
> Of invariableness of justice
> Our glorious founder
> Heracles gave us,
> Son loved of Zeus his father—for he sinn'd,
>
> And the strand of Euboea,
> And the promontory of Cenaeum,
> His painful, solemn
> Punishment witness'd,
> Beheld his expiation—for he died.

Arnold wanted to convey to the English reader the "grand effects" of Greek tragedy as he felt Goethe had conveyed them to German readers with his *Iphigeneia*. With unconscious humor he expressed to "K" his enthusiastic objective for *Merope*: "I think and hope it will have what Buddha called the 'character of *Fixity*, that true sign of the Law.' "²¹ In this sterile play he achieved something very like A. E. Housman's justly celebrated parody of translated plays, *Fragment of a Greek Tragedy*.

III   *Oxford Lectures*

Arnold's appointment as foreign assistant commissioner to the Duke of Newcastle's Commission took him to the Continent for five months in the spring and summer of 1859. He visited Mme. de Staël, he dined at Lady Elgin's with Sainte-Beuve, he talked with Guizot and Lacordaire on education, with Renan on the Celtic race, and with Lord Cowley and with French citizens whom he met by chance, on the state of French and Austrian affairs. Educational issues alone did not absorb his interest in a year in which Austria was at war with France and Sardinia, and when the settlement at Villafranca on July 8 left much of Italy under Austrian power. To Arnold's disquiet, England stood apart from the crisis; so, while he was abroad, Arnold composed his thoughts in his pamphlet *England and the Italian Question,* which was published in August, 1859. Lionel Trilling regards the pamphlet not only as an expression of Arnold's opposition to England's aloofness but also of his sense that literature has a mission to guide the "idea moved masses" in a time when democracy was increasing and when the power of an English aristocracy, whose past achievement he admired, was fading.[22] In some way this pamphlet must have satisfied Arnold's vague hankering to prod the political conscience of his country. This desire he satisfied more fully only many years later, for he now turned to the more congenial area of critical taste.

On November 3, 1860, Arnold delivered at Oxford what he termed in a letter to his mother "an off lecture."[23] He regarded as his main course of lectures the series on the Modern Element in Literature. The lecture was on Homer. He expanded his ideas in two additional lectures and published all three in 1861 as *On Translating Homer.* Their polemical character evoked a response from Francis W. Newman, a translator of Homer and the brother of John Henry Newman. Arnold in turn replied on November 30, 1861, with a fourth lecture, which he printed independently as *On Translating Homer. Last Words* (1862).

The initial lecture in this series began innocently with a modest intimation of Arnold's qualifications to speak on the subject: "It has more than once been suggested to me that I should translate Homer. That is a task for which I have neither the time nor the courage; but the suggestion led me to regard yet more closely a poet whom I had already long studied, . . ."[24] However, he undertook to demonstrate the special qualities of Homer that he said must be conveyed if one is not to fall short in translation as F. W. Newman had recently done with the *Iliad* and as I. C. Wright was currently doing. The qualities are rapidity, plainness, and directness in thought; plainness and directness in substance; and nobility.

In addition to the appearance of several current translations, there was contemporary interest in the academic controversy over Homeric metre and in Friedrich Wolf's theory that claimed multiple authorship for the Homeric poems. In giving this series of lectures, Arnold enjoyed the advantage of a subject that was familiar and appropriate to the Oxford lectureship and to his cultivated audience, and yet he was able to skirt the thickets of academic controversy to illuminate the nature of what for him was a more essential theme: the nature and effect of *the grand style.*

Arnold initially avoids defining the grand style, but he does say "that the presence or absence of the grand style can only be spiritually discerned."[25] For the time being he rests with defining it by illustrations, the "touchstone" device of the later essay "The Study of Poetry" (1880). It is, however, already clear that the touchstones exhibit not only simplicity and lucidity of expression, but they almost invariably recall a moment of pathos or a context in which a noble ethical attitude is exhibited, either by some stoical choice or by profoundly inward religious acquiescence. For example, there are Achilles' words to Lykaon:

ἀλλά, φίλος, θάνε καὶ σύ· τίη ὀλυφύρεαι οὕτως;
κάτθανε καὶ Πάτροκλος, ὅπερ σέο πολλὸν ἀμείνων,

("Be content, good friend, die also thou! why lamentest thou thyself on this wise? Patroclus, too, died, who was a far better than thou."—*Iliad,* xxi. 106).

Or there is Dante's pitying response to three noble Florentine suicides,

Lascio lo fele, e vo per dolci pomi
Promessi a me per lo verace Duca;
Ma fino al centro pria convien ch'io tomi,

("I leave the gall of bitterness, and I go for the apples of sweetness promised unto me by my faithful Guide; but far as the centre it behoves me first to fall."—*Hell*, xvi. 61).

By spiritual discernment in literary matters Arnold means something more than tact and taste, although it includes them; spiritual discernment also means a refinement of moral sensibility. Arnold's esthetic is conceived in terms of a sensibility that unifies, in T. S. Eliot's phrase, thought and feeling. Sensuous perception and ethical perception have equal parts.

Arnold formulates his definition of the grand style in the last —and liveliest—lecture on Homer. The definition echoes Longinus, for Arnold admits that the nobility must be in the poet as well as in the subject matter and in the style. "I think it will be found," he says, "that the grand style arises in poetry, *when a noble nature, poetically gifted, treats with simplicity or with severity a serious subject.*"[26] When he speaks of "severity" and "simplicity," it is difficult not to feel that he has in mind what, in "The Literary Influence of Academies," he calls "the *ethical* influences of style in language."[27]

Arnold's prose in general is polemical in its origin; and, however disguised by urbanity and elegance, it is controversial in its character. In the lectures on Homer Arnold maintained towards his main subject the disinterestedness which is part of the critical endeavor in any field. But towards F. W. Newman especially, as well as towards other contemporaries, he employs the talent for sarcasm and the sallies of ironic humor that exasperated the many victims of his Dunciad, but that sometimes reward the modern reader of his most unpromisingly pedestrian articles.

In 1850 Arnold had read Newman's *Phases of Faith*, and he wrote to Clough: "F. Newman's book I saw yestern at our ouse. He seems to have written himself down an hass."[28] While the assertion is not repeated in the lectures on Homer, the implications are plain in his damaging analysis. One elaborately contrived passage may suffice to convey the tenor. Arnold writes:

Coleridge says, in his strange language, speaking of the union of the human soul with the divine essence, that this takes place

Whene'er the mist, which stands 'twixt God and thee,
Defecates to a pure transparency;

and so, too, it may be said of that union of the translator with his original, which alone can produce a good translation, that it takes place when the mist which stands between them—the mist of alien modes of thinking, speaking, and feeling on the translator's part—"defecates to a pure transparency and disappears."[29]

Arnold does not find this union in Newman; for, he says, ". . . between Mr. Newman and Homer is interposed a cloud of more than Egyptian thickness,—namely a manner, in Mr. Newman's version, eminently ignoble, while Homer's manner is eminently noble." And Arnold proceeds with a devastating choice of quotations to prove his point.

With a touch of anguished snobbery, Arnold delivers his final rebuff to Newman. To reproach those who have reproached him for the offense he may have given by his witty sallies, Arnold borrows the Chesterfieldian response of Antoine Rivarol: "Ah! no one considers how much pain every man of taste has had to *suffer,* before he ever inflicts any."[30]

IV *Essays in Criticism* (1865)

The lectures and the education reports kept Arnold, he wrote his mother, from "feeling starved and shrunk up."[31] They also enlarged his reputation, as did his poetry. Even on the circuit he traveled with Judge Wightman, he said in 1861 that he found "people are beginning to know something about *me* myself, but I am still far oftener an object of interest as his [Dr. Arnold's] son than on my own account."[32] He was subject to the publicity of hostile comment, for example in the essay "Homeric Translators and Critics" that appeared in the *Saturday Review* for July 27, 1861. And he enjoyed the publicity of favorable comment also; he wrote to Lady de Rothschild, who had called his attention to an article in the *Westminster Review* for October, 1863: "It contains so much praise that you must have thought I wrote it myself, except that I should hardly have called myself by the hideous title of 'Professor.' "[33]

His worlds of social acquaintance were also enlarging: in Oxford and in public education, his circle grew through his official positions; in the sphere of politics, he added friends through his sister "K"'s husband, William E. Forster; in the county families, through Judge Wightman; among the "Barbarians," through Sir Anthony and Lady de Rothschild, whose hospitableness at their country house at Aston Clinton figures charmingly in his family correspondence. On June 28, 1862, before going to Oxford to deliver the Creweian oration, he wrote a letter to his mother that conveys a sense of his social activity:

The Vice-Chancellor has asked me to dine with him on Tuesday, and he has a great party afterwards. This is almost official, and I do so little as an Oxford Professor that I do not like to decline; besides, I shall probably meet Lord Palmerston at the dinner. . . . Our dinner-party last night went off very well. I think I told you the Lingens were coming. They were both very amiable, and not the least allusion was made to the Code. To-night we have Chief Justice Erle, the Seniors, the Froudes, the Forsters, Drummond Wolff, and Montagu Blackett. We went after our party last night to the Seniors, and found Thackeray there, who was very amusing, kissing his hand to Flu [Arnold's wife], and calling me a monster, but adding that 'he had told all to her father.' He asked us to dinner for to-morrow, Sunday, but we are engaged to the Forsters. We also met the Brookfields there, and we dine with them on Monday. I do nothing except my inspection, eat and drink much more than I wish to, and long for the circuit to bring me a little country air and peace. . . . On Wednesday we met the Grant Duffs.[34]

Arnold's relative "nothing" in 1862 was followed by the very fruitful year of 1863, and for the next two and a half decades, without remission of his professional duties or sociableness, he energetically produced lectures, periodical essays, books, and reviews of books. From the lectures and reviews written in 1863 and 1864, he made a selection for *Essays in Criticism* (1865). He thought of *essay* in the old meaning, that is, "attempt—specimen."[35] The cosmopolitanism of Arnold—which, like his Classical taste and his admiration for a Chesterfieldian aristocracy of manner, reminds us of his strong yet overlooked connection with eighteenth-century ideals—is evident in the range of these essays: "The Function of Criticism at the Present Time," "The Literary Influence of Academies," "Maurice de Guérin," "Eugénie de Guérin," "Heinrich Heine," "Pagan and Medieval Religious Sentiment," "Joubert," "Spinoza," "Marcus Aurelius."

Diverse though the essays are, they develop leading ideas that connect to give the book an inner consistency. There is, after all, a high degree of thematic coherence and consistency of purpose throughout Arnold's prose work. He himself was struck by "the sort of unity that as a book to stimulate the better humanity in us the volume has."[36] The critical concerns of *Essays in Criticism*, for example, are as often spiritual and social as they are literary; they parallel the objectives he set forth for middle-class education in *A French Eton;* and they broaden into the themes of *Culture and Anarchy* in the next few years. As we read Arnold, the effect is one of continuing discourse. Repeatedly the point of departure is a quotation from himself or an allusion to some position taken earlier. Constantly the aim is the increasing humanization of individuals and of society.

The brilliant essay, "The Function of Criticism at the Present Time," which stands first in Arnold's sequence of arrangement, begins with a quotation from his second lecture in *On Translating Homer*: "Of the literature of France and Germany, as of the intellect of Europe in general, the main effort, for now many years has been a critical effort; the endeavour, in all branches of knowledge, theology, philosophy, history, art, science, to see the object as in itself it really is."[37] To see the object thus one must train oneself in the discipline of *disinterestedness*, of detachment, of objectivity so that one can see, in the field of letters, the special configuration of a writer, as Arnold attempts to do in the case of the de Guérins and of Marcus Aurelius, or so that one can admit in the face of loudly proclaimed achievement (the English Romantic poets) or of popular values (complacency in material values, Philistinism) the intellectual and spiritual limitations of even one's own time and nation. The detachment necessary to the critical effort is not itself the final goal. For Arnold defines criticism as *"a disinterested endeavour to learn and propagate the best that is known and thought in the world."*[38]

Although Arnold was aware of the intellectual concern of his age with ideas about change, progress, and development—or about being as a mode of becoming—and, although in his religious essays of the 1870's he directly confronted some of them, he inclines to a belief in the absolute in his literary criticism. Despite the poetic statements that imply that, as individuals, we are ringed about by a wall of subjective personality, he strives for objectivity and detachment in criticism. Arnold assumes that there are absolute standards in literary judgment, and his position contrasts sharply with that of the relativistic and subjective Walter Pater, who seizes one of Arnold's phrases to sharpen the differences between them. In Pater's Preface to *Studies in the History of the Renaissance* (1873), he said: " 'To see the object as in itself it really is,' has been justly said to be the aim of all true criticism whatever; and in aesthetic criticism the first step toward seeing one's object as it really is, is to know one's own impression as it really is, to discriminate it, to realise it distinctly."

Arnold's definition of criticism as "a disinterested endeavour to learn and propagate the best that is known and thought in the world" gives to criticism an educative purpose and asks it to make judgments of value about substantive content. "Best" for Arnold is both an esthetic and a moralistic term. If "Wragg, poor thing!" did not exist by the Ilissus, if the *Edinburgh Review* and the *Quarterly Review* and the *British Quarterly Review* do exist as partisan organs and not like the *Revue des Deux Mondes* "for a play of the mind," and if England reads Bishop Colenso on the Pentateuch while France reads Ernest Renan's *Vie de Jésus,* it is because Athens and Paris represent esthetic and intellectual cultivation—cultivation of an aspect of character that does not regard practical results as its absolute good as does the British Philistine.

In *Essays in Criticism* the limitations of the English mind are frequently exposed by measuring it with the French intellect. "There is in France," Arnold says in his essay on Joubert, "a sympathy with intellectual activity for its own sake, and for the sake of its inherent pleasurableness and beauty, keener than any which exists in England." The praise of French intellectuality, of a country whose masses are "idea-moved," whose people have "a conscience in intellectual matters," is a theme of the volume that is incidental at times but one that assumes major importance in "The Literary Influence of Academies." This essay, detached and dispassionate in tone, seems to concentrate on demonstrating the value for the intellectual conscience of having a central authority in matters of style; but in effect it treats another leading theme of *Essays in Criticism*: the limitations of the British middle class. Honesty and energy the English have as their national traits—but they exhibit provincialism in thought and expression; they make a merit of the willfulness of going one's own way and of doing as one likes; they are beset by "the two great banes of humanity. . . . self-conceit and the laziness coming from self-conceit."

The war upon the Philistines, the middle class, whose apostle for Arnold was Lord Macaulay and whose vehicle was the London *Times,* is continuously being waged openly or subtly in the *Essays in Criticism.* The assault is open in "The Function of Criticism," and also in "Heinrich Heine," where Heine's term *Philistine,* that Carlyle had already imported, is issued current again. Despite the seeming claim for an absolute disinterestedness, Arnold's disinterestedness is relative to his long-range educative design.

Perceptively discussing *Essays in Criticism* for the *North American Review,* Henry James regretted that, "when Heine is for once in a way seriously spoken of, he should not be spoken of more as the great poet which he is, and which even in New England he will one day be admitted to be, than with reference to the great moralist which he is not, and which he never claimed to be."[39] When Arnold reads Heine's line of activity as " 'a soldier in the war of liberation of humanity,' " it is essentially of an intellectual and not of a political deliverance that he is thinking. Heine is represented as a continuator of Goethe, whose "profound, imperturbable naturalism is absolutely fatal to all routine thinking."[40] Although Arnold may disinterestedly present Heine to the reader as Arnold really sees him, he also characteristically uses him to attack " 'ächt britische Beschränktheit,' as he calls it,—the *genuine British narrowness.*" He elaborates for his own purpose Heine's attack on William Cobbett: "Our Cobbett is thus for him, much as he disliked our clergy and aristocracy whom Cobbett attacked, a Philistine with six fingers on every hand and on every foot six toes, four-and-twenty in number: a Philistine, the staff of whose spear is like a weaver's beam."[41]

Arnold was not prompted to his long engagement with the Philistines by fierce indignation or by despair, but by a belief that they needed education and that they were educable. He was at bottom confident about the middle class. A very few months before he composed "The Literary Influence of Academies" for its initial use as an Oxford lecture in June, 1864, he wrote in a very important letter to Richard Cobden:

I believe, with Toqueville, that the multitude is most miserable in countries where there is a great aristocracy and I believe that in modern societies a great aristocracy is a retarding and stupifying element, but our aristocracy will not modify itself and English society along with itself; our lower class will not modify them, and one can hardly wish it should, as things are, for it would be a *jacquerie*; our middle class, as things are, has in my opinion neither the wisdom nor the power to modify them. I know our liberal politicians think higher than I do of our middle class as it at present exists; I have seen a good deal of it from my connection with dissenting schools, and I am convinced that till its mind is a great deal more open, and its spirit a great deal freer and higher, it will never prevail against the aristocratic class which has certain very considerable merits and forces of its own; and it will not perhaps, deserve to prevail against it. At the same time there is undoubtedly just now a ferment in the spirit of the middle class which I see nowhere else, and which seems to me the greatest power and *purchase* we have; and all that can be done to open their minds and to strengthen them by a better culture should I think be done; we shall then have a real force to employ against the aristocratic force and a moving force against an inert and unprogressive force, a force of ideas against the less spiritual force of established power, antiquity, prestige, and social refinement.[42]

Arnold believed that the "true mode of intellectual action" is "persuasion, the instilment of conviction." He saw a generation of the middle class "with new impulses astir in them, more freedom and accessibility of spirit; it is on them one must work—in literature, at least."[43]

Perhaps the most pervasive theme of the *Essays in Criticism*—as it is the subtlest—is Arnold's insistence on the importance of achieving a balance between the heart and sentiment, on the one hand, and between the senses and imagination, on the other; between pagan and Christian religious sentiment; between Monte Alverno and Pompeii; and between extremes of spirit of which Hebraism and Hellenism are the expression. Between these poles the balance is achieved by what Arnold calls "the imaginative reason."[44] The Greek poets "from Pindar to Sophocles" possessed it, and it makes for right thinking and right conduct. Its literary expression makes literature a criticism of life.

Disinterestedness is needed, but not that alone, to win the spirit that connects these poles. In addition, the imaginative reason gains the victory over Philistinism; it makes possible the emotion and spiritual refinement of a Marcus Aurelius; it leaves behind—in the language of one of Arnold's favorite phrases from Goethe: "was uns alle bändigt, DAS GEMEINE"—what confines us all, the commonplace.[45]

Essays in Criticism remains from any point of view one of the three or four essential books by Arnold because of the variety of the ideas and of the methods he employs for incitement or persuasion, either in the strategic design of whole essays, or in stylistic devices employed within them. Space does not permit analysis of them, but we cannot think of the Arnold of these essays without thinking of his jocular and telling adaptation of Quintilian's categories of style: Corinthian, Asiatic, Attic; his irony—"the best breed in the world"; his facetiousness and sense for farce—the lugubrious fun with the murderer Müller and the Bow tragedy in the Preface; his mockery and satire—the play with Adderley and Roebuck; his phrase making—"to see the object as in itself it really is"; his vein of sentiment—Oxford "spreading her gardens to the moonlight"; his passionate appeals for integrity—"Périssons en résistant."

V On the Study of Celtic Literature

On the Study of Celtic Literature (1867) is the final book that was made directly from the lectures for the Oxford professorship. They had an intermediate life in Thackeray's *Cornhill Magazine* in 1866. From the opening antitheses between Llandudno and Liverpool, Celt and Saxon, sentiment and energy,

Arnold makes his way with great tact and quiet charm through tracts of philology and of theories about racial characteristics and racial affinity, through analysis of the Titanism, the melancholy, and the magic of Celtic poetry. In pursuing his way, he is motivated by his wish to be disinterested on the side of literary criticism; but on the side of practice he wishes to strike a blow against Philistinism and to make a plea "to found at Oxford a chair of Celtic, and to send, through the gentle ministration of science, a message of peace to Ireland."[46]

For the book form of the lectures Arnold composed a graceful yet lively preface, developed on grounds central to his main effort. "My friend, Mr. Goldwin Smith, says, in his eloquent way, that England is the favourite of Heaven. Far be it from me to say that England is not the favourite of Heaven; but at this moment she reminds me more of what the prophet Isaiah calls 'a bull in a net.' "[47] Let us substitute, he concludes, "in place of that type of Englishman with whom alone the Celt has too long been familiar, a new type, more intelligent, more gracious, and more humane."[48]

Early in 1867 Arnold met the aged Henry Crabb Robinson in the Athenaeum. "He asked me," Arnold wrote his mother, "which of all my books I should myself name as the one that had got me 'my great reputation,' as he wanted to buy it. I said I had not 'a great reputation,' upon which he answered: 'Then it is some other Matthew Arnold who writes the books.' "[49]

The decade of the professorship consolidated Arnold's reputation both as to his interests and his style. "And," said the impressionable young American Henry Adams, "Adams thought Arnold the best form of expression in his time."[50]

CHAPTER 6

Anarchy and Authority

I New Poems

THE final lecture of the Oxford professorship was "Culture and Its Enemies." It was delivered on June 7, 1867, and printed in the *Cornhill Magazine* for July. In July *New Poems* was also published. This was, in effect, Arnold's final volume of poetry; for, in the several new editions of his poetry that subsequently appeared during his lifetime, there were revivals of a few magazine pieces, rearrangements, textual revisions, but only a very few new poems. The most important of these is "Westminster Abbey," an elegy for A. P. Stanley, the dean of Westminster and the biographer of Arnold's father.

New Poems revived "Empedocles on Etna," at the request of Robert Browning, as well as several short poems from *The Strayed Reveller*. "The Scholar-Gipsy" was reprinted to accompany its companion poem "Thyrsis," which had been published as the leading contribution in *Macmillan's Magazine* in April, 1866. A few other poems, most importantly "Stanzas from the Grande Chartreuse" (*Fraser's Magazine*, April, 1855), were reprinted from periodicals. There were also some thirty new poems, ranging in quality from fourteen rather turgid Wordsworthian sonnets to triumphs like "Palladium" and "Dover Beach," which he may have written as early as 1851.

During the twenty-odd years of Arnold's poetic activity, some failures of expression persist. The notorious line "Who prop, thou ask'st, in these bad days, my mind?" from the 1849 volume can be matched in 1867 with "Thou mak'st the heaven thou hop'st indeed thy home." The occasional banal epithet, like "German Weimar" of "Stanzas in Memory of the Author of Obermann," recurs as in "German Aarau" in the third sonnet on the tragic actress "Rachel." When confronted with a line like "Germany, France, Christ, Moses, Athens, Rome," the reader recalls wonderingly Arnold's claims about the "grand moral effects of style." The sonnet "The Austerity of Poetry" affords the epitome of bathos, or the art of sinking in poetry: "A prop gave way! crash fell a platform! lo." But, if *New Poems* affords examples of Arnold's persistent blunders, the book also illustrates his power to concentrate in the symbolism of "Dover Beach" and "Palladium" thoughts and feelings concerning isolation, the rarity of mutual love, the *condition humaine,* the "damned times," and the integrity of the buried life that in earlier poems he had treated sometimes more sentimentally or more diffusely.

New Poems gives final expression to Arnold's earlier wistfulness and to his current sense of purposefulness in "the world's new hour" for himself and for society. "Stanzas from the Grande Chartreuse" of 1855 evokes with charming Romantic melancholy a sadly Arcadian image of Alpine meadows filled with autumn crocuses and "soft-suffused/ With rain"; and, while the poet's rational being knows the impossibility for him of retreat to a Newmanesque faith, his emotional being grasps the force of his alienation: "Wandering between two worlds, one dead,/ The other powerless to be born." The poet, who once confessed to his friend Ernest Fontanès his weakness for the historical religions,[1] identifies himself imaginatively with the Carthusians; he softens the severity of their ascetic withdrawal to something like the melancholy that surrounds his Iseult of Brittany—

> We are like children rear'd in shade
> Beneath some old-world abbey wall,
> Forgotten in a forest-glade,
> And secret from the eyes of all.

From the material advances of the nineteenth century ("You give the universe your law,/ You triumph over time and space!") and from the medieval pageants of war and hunt that stand for society, the Carthusians, as Arnold wished to do, turn to a quest for inward peace.

Arnold, however, had learned that a profound inwardness was not incompatible with the world of activity. The Palladium coexists with "the battle in the plain." The Obermann of the 1852 volume urged resistance, not merely icy despair. In the "Obermann Once More" of 1867 the spirit of Senancour's hero takes a wide survey of European history to instruct the poet as to his duties in a modern world in which social ills afflict multitudes. They have "need of joy!/ But joy whose grounds are true," and the poet must help to create " *One common wave of thought and joy/ Lifting mankind again!*" With this inner illumination the poet wakes from his vision to a real and hopeful world of Alpine heights on which he sees "the morning break."

Perhaps it was in some degree the polemical motive for the elegiac "Rugby Chapel," the effort it deliberately made to counter Fitzjames Stephen's disparaging view of Dr. Thomas Arnold, that reduces to the didactic this well-known poem in which the symbolic father, "Cheerful, and helpful, and firm," marshals men to their goal. On the other hand "Thyrsis," Arnold's deeply personal elegy for his friend Clough, presents, in the "fugitive and gracious light" and in the gipsy scholar who seeks it, moving symbols for the steadfastness and hopefulness of the quest for a serene and humanistic way of life.[2] Deriving from the great pastoral tradition of Theocritus and Milton, "Thyrsis" benefits from the detachment which the ceremonies of pastoral elegy afford. Arnold wanted the diction of this poem "to be so artless as to be almost heedless." It is sufficient for his purposes of evocation that bluebells are "trembling," fritillaries "white" or "purple," and that sweet-william has "his homely cottage-smell." Arnold's descriptions recall rather than create sensuous experience. They are in sharp contrast to the descriptions, for example, of his younger contemporary Gerard Manley Hopkins with his "rose moles all in stipple upon trout that swim" or "Fresh firecoal chestnut-falls."

It is a commonplace to say of "Thyrsis"—as of "Lycidas" or "Adonais"—that there is less of the mourned in the poem than there is of the mourner. But elegy is not obituary; and the formalism of the pastoral with its lamentation, change of mood, and consolation gave Arnold a congenial vehicle for his statement of the existential dilemma. In "Thyrsis" the solution is just intimated in the cheerful duty of pursuing a quest. More fully stated, this solution was to proclaim a humanistic and joyful morality, not the absurdity of the human situation. Arnold had, after all, created in his Empedocles a figure whose analysis of life reduced it to the absurd and whose conclusion led him to the absurdity of self-destruction.

Arnold was aware of the media and the styles that he believed would best convey his thought. There was little more to convey by poetry. He was aware of the new audiences he wished to reach by prose, although his successes were by no means always complete. Yet the wish to be a poet lingered. In August, 1861, he sent a message to his sister: "Tell Fan I must finish off for the present my critical writings between this and forty, and give the next ten years earnestly to poetry. It is my last chance."[3] We think of poor Dencombe in Henry James's story "The Middle Years"; for, except for "Thyrsis," "Palladium," and "Obermann Once More," Arnold's best poetical work was done; he had had his first and only chance. But we perceive through Arnold's letters—as well as from the evident joy in the endeavor that enters into the formal prose discourses—his increasing sense of exhilaration as he pursues his critical and controversial work.

In 1863 he wrote, "It is very animating to think that one at last has a chance of *getting at* the English public. Such a public as it is, and such work as one wants to do with it!"[4] Regarding *A French Eton*, he said, "I really want to *persuade* on this subject, and I have felt how necessary it was to keep down many and many sharp and telling things that rise to one's lips, and which one would gladly utter if one's object was to show one's own abilities."[5] In 1866 he told his mother, "I more and more become conscious of having something to do, and of a resolution to do it."[6] As the ideas he had for a single essay on anarchy and authority expanded into a second and a third, he asked George Smith if there were an objection to a third; and he hoped he need not bridle his "fine frenzy."[7] Before he had finished, his enthusiasm for his subject led him to write a fourth and a fifth essay.

His buoyancy was expressed in his anticipation of the public reception of the 1865 volume of *Essays in Criticism*: "Then, of course, if this book succeeds, the way is the more clear for my bringing in my favourite notions yet further; if I can only, as Marcus Aurelius says, keep 'the balance true, and my mind

even.'"⁸ Arnold rejoiced some years later to hear from the
Orientalist E. O. M. Deutsch "that he was distinctly conscious,
while writing his article on the Talmud, that if it had not been
for what I had done he could not have written that article in
the *Quarterly,* and the British public could not have read it."⁹

Arnold increasingly found his line of endeavor in areas where
his talent in poetry could not reach. Although his talent was
larger than that of A. E. Housman, it was circumscribed, as
Housman's was, in its range. Arnold's best poems express the
dilemma of man's existential isolation; the fullest poetic statements of Arnold's solution to that dilemma, on the other hand,
tend towards the didacticism of "Rugby Chapel." His talent
for satire, which laughs out in a restricted way in a few verses
in *New Poems,* finds its full voice in *Friendship's Garland* and
animates much of the more formal prose as it does his correspondence. The poetic sensibility that pronounced on Dryden
and Pope the judgment that they "are not classics of our poetry,
they are classics of our prose" was not likely, after all, to find in
verse an outlet for his often satirical way of seeing things. In
New Poems the vein of satire is about exhausted with the
Horatian characterizations in "A Wish," the Clough-like ironic
turns of "Pis-Aller," the opening verses of Part II of "Bacchanalia," and the wry quatrain "A Caution to Poets":

> What poets feel not, when they make,
> A pleasure in creating,
> The World, in *its* turn, will not take
> Pleasure in contemplating.

II *Culture and Anarchy*

Although Empedocles may choose the crater, society persists
in organizing itself and in perpetuating itself. Man, therefore,
must live a dual role; he has a commitment to himself and to
society. To analyze the nature of man's commitment and to
reconcile the dual claims, Arnold turned to the resources of
prose discourse. The early essay "The Function of Criticism at
the Present Time" examined a literary concern, but it also developed a social one. The full statement of Arnold's social con-

cern was developed in his six essays for the *Cornhill Magazine* in 1867 and 1868. Arnold called the *Cornhill* essays "Anarchy and Authority," but for book publication he gave them the softened and more persuasive title *Cuture and Anarchy*. The scope of the essays was suggested by the subtitle *An Essay in Political and Social Criticism*. The Preface, in which Arnold acquiesced with the judgments of Thackeray and George Smith that he had done his "d——d-st," was finally ready early in January, 1869; and the book was published late that month.[10]

He sent copies to Lady de Rothschild and Benjamin Disraeli, among others. By June he was pleased to hear that the Princess Alice, Queen Victoria's second daughter, was "quite fascinated with my *Culture and Anarchy*, uses all its phrases, and knows long bits by heart."[11] "You will see," he wrote his mother, "that it will have a considerable effect in the end, and the chapters on Hellenism and Hebraism are in the main, I am convinced, so true that they will form a kind of centre for English thought and speculation on the matters treated in them."[12]

By anarchy, Arnold understood outward manifestations of disorder, like the National Reform League assembly in Trafalgar Square; the Fenian attack on Clerkenwell Prison in December, 1867; or the new American religion Mormonism, that extravagant example of proliferating and proudly dissident sects. By anarchy, he also meant inward signs; specifically, these were "the want of sensitiveness of intellectual conscience, the disbelief in right reason, [and] the dislike of authority" that characterized for him the typical Englishman.[13] By culture, on the other hand, he meant authority—the authority of a national church and of the state, hypostatized as "the best self" of the nation; he also meant inward ripeness, the Socratic admonition "Know thyself," and the admonition of Jesus "Be ye therefore perfect."

In either condition—anarchy or culture—the inner disposition determines the outer. Tirelessly, Arnold works variations on his theme "Except a man be born *from above*, he cannot have part in the society of the future."[14] His rhetorical phrases—"the springs of conduct," "the totality of man," "the main current of human life," "the law of human progress"—are meaningful in terms of certain convictions. Arnold believed that in the flux of change there remain constant values of human morality (in the words of Sophocles' Chorus in *Oedipus the King*, "The god in them is strong, and grows not old"); they are discoverable through "right reason" or "imaginative reason"; they are attainable as a way of conduct by developing the "totality" of our nature. "Culture" is Arnold's term for the balanced development of the intellectual side and the religious side; in other words, it is his term for the individual pursuit of spiritual perfection. In its collective operation, culture is the agency that will overcome "the want of ideas of its aristocratic class, the provincial narrowness and vulgarity of its middle class, and the nonage of its lower."[15]

Both "culture" and "perfection" are words fraught with semantic dangers. When Arnold himself in the Preface (1869) to *Culture and Anarchy* regrets the lack in the United States of "effective centers of high culture," he perilously invites the identification of culture with a Pateresque estheticism, or with a leisured and social exclusiveness. When he calls harmonious perfection "the true way of salvation," he eventually invites man to ask himself perilous questions about his own attained measure of perfection: ". . . the worth of what a man thinks about God and the objects of religion depends upon what the man *is*; and what the man *is*, depends upon his having more or less reached the measure of a perfect and total man."[16] We ask rather, borrowing Arnold's own remarkable phrase, "Where shall we find language innocent enough" to express publicly the private aspect of Arnold's mission?[17]

In "Culture: a Dialogue" in the *Fortnightly Review* (November, 1867) Frederic Harrison, the young Positivist, wittily exposed Arnold's not entirely satisfactory definition of culture, and the self-satisfied tone that undermines at times his effectiveness. Harrison is writing not only with "Sweetness and Light" in mind, but also the satirical pursuit of the theme Arnold had begun to make in 1866 in the letters to the *Pall Mall Gazette* that he later collected as *Friendship's Garland*. In Harrison's parody, Arnold's Arminius inquires about culture and human ideals:

"But how does it recognize these," he asked helplessly, evidently now striking at random, "if it has neither system, method, nor logic?"
"By Insight," I replied triumphantly; "by its own inborn sensibility to beauty, truth, and life."

"But if a man is born without it?" he asked.

"God help him then," I rejoined, "for I cannot"; and as Arminius was still silent, I hummed gaily to myself, "Sordid, unfeeling, reprobate, degraded, spiritless outcast"; and indeed there are but too many in that plight.[18]

Arnold told Lady de Rothschild, "You will be amused, as I have been, with Mr. Harrison's answer to me in the *Fortnightly*. It is scarcely the least vicious, and in parts so amusing that I laughed till I cried."[19]

The Oxford lecture "Culture and Its Enemies," renamed "Sweetness and Light," became the first chapter of *Culture and Anarchy*. Adapting Swift's metaphor of the bee from *The Battle of the Books*, Arnold makes sweetness stand for beauty of character; light, for intelligence. But light has additional connotations of spiritual illumination that lend an emotional value beyond a rationalistic sense of intelligence. Together, sweetness and light compose the inward condition of culture, a condition "at variance with the mechanical and material civilization in esteem with us."

The presence of dissolvent forces breaking down old institutions led Arnold earlier to the despair of "Empedocles on Etna"; he now confronts them with the cheering sense that the iron forces of adhesion to the old and exclusion of the new have "wonderfully yielded" to the pressure of the Time-Spirit. The middle classes seem more malleable; the reform bill of 1867 has released the new and incalculable force of democracy. Arnold's cheerfulness is fortified by a belief that this is the historic "moment for culture to be of service"; it is also fortified by his increasing stress on a beneficent *tendency* in things, that there is a "universal order which seems to be intended and aimed at in the world."[20]

Hence Arnold opens his campaign in "Sweetness and Light" against "faith in machinery," against mistaking means for ends, against the divisiveness of sectarianism arrogantly proclaiming as an ideal "the Dissidence of Dissent and the Protestantism of the Protestant religion," against violent rejection of the past in favor of abstract systems of social renovation. And he directs the campaign with his great resources of persuasion—the appeal to "the Oxford of the past"—and of satire and satirical understatement:

So, after hearing Bentham cried loudly up as the renovator of modern society, and Bentham's mind and ideas proposed as the rulers of our future, I open the *Deontology*. There I read: "While Xenophon was writing his history and Euclid teaching geometry, Socrates and Plato were talking nonsense under pretence of teaching wisdom and morality. This morality of theirs consisted in words; this wisdom of theirs was the denial of matters known to every man's experience." From the moment of reading that, I am delivered from the bondage of Bentham! the fanaticism of his adherents can touch me no longer.[21]

The second essay, "Doing as One Likes," balances the limited ideal of personal liberty, which, if undirected, is anarchy, against the interests and authority of the State—"the nation in its collective and corporate charcter."[22] The willfulness of personal liberty as an ideal end in itself is wonderfully exemplified by Arnold's grasp of the absurd facts of his society: the erection of Cole's Truss Manufactory in Trafalgar Square, or "That beautiful sentence Sir Daniel Gooch quoted to the Swindon workmen, and which I treasure as Mrs. Gooch's Golden Rule, or the Divine Injunction 'Be ye Perfect' done into British,—the sentence Sir Daniel Gooch's mother repeated to him every morning when he was a boy going to work:—'*Ever remember, my dear Dan, that you should look forward to being some day manager of that concern!*' "[23]

"Barbarians, Philistines, Populace" elaborates Arnold's now-famous classification of English society: the aristocracy, with its capability for "a high, chivalrous style" but its "fierce turn for resistance" and inaccessibility to ideas; the middle class with its honesty and energy, but provincialism and narrowness; and the "vast residuum," the working class emergent as a force to augment the middle class, but as yet undeveloped, "marching where it likes, meeting where it likes, bawling what it likes, breaking what it likes."[24] How shall one woo these classes to prefer the aims of a Wilhelm von Humboldt: "first, to perfect one's self by all the means in one's power, and secondly, to try and create in the world around one an aristocracy, the most numerous that one possibly could, of talents and characters"?[25]

One is aided in this effort by learning to see things as in themselves they really are, by developing "curiosity" and "disinterestedness" in Arnold's intellectual sense of those terms. One may begin by recognizing the overbalance in the English character of Hebraism, or strictness of conscience, and by recognizing the need for Hellenism, or spontaneity of conscience, the need to cultivate intellectual and esthetic sensibilities. This is the theme of the fourth essay, "Hebraism and Hellenism." The great society is the one in which one can say without sensing an incongruity that "Socrates is terribly *at ease in Zion.*"[26] Man's efforts in this direction are for Arnold remarkably aided by the Time-Spirit: "For more than two hundred years the main stream of man's advance has moved towards knowing himself and the world, seeing things as they are, spontaneity of consciousness."[27]

England has worked against the tendency. Therefore there is one thing needful, "Porro Unum est Necessarium," which is the title he gave to the fifth essay. The one thing needful, it is no secret, is Hellenism. Arnold extends the ideas of the preceding essay. He is bent upon showing the flexibility, the Hellenism of temper in St. Paul. Puritanism stresses the Pauline idea of resurrection after death. It is needful to perceive that it equally means being born again in the present, so that one can have a part in the social order of man's earthly future. From this high ground Arnold returns, like the poet's muse in "Lycidas" when St. Peter's "dread voice is past," to traverse the very mundane world of the Real Estate Intestacy Bill and the Deceased Wife's Sister Bill and Nonconformist fears of church establishments, in the final essay of *Culture and Anarchy,* "Our Liberal Practitioners." He returns also to another aid for perfecting society, namely, the agency of the state: *"The State is of the religion of all its citizens, without the fanaticism of any of them."*[28] He not only resumes his satirical posture towards the Philistines and recognizes on abstract grounds the civilizing force of the state, but he also emphasizes with immediate practicalness the grave needs of East London with its underfed, disease-infested, uneducated, and incredibly multiplying population.

III *Friendship's Garland*

Concurrently with the composition of the essays that became *Culture and Anarchy,* Arnold was engaged in writing at irregular intervals for the *Pall Mall Gazette* a series of gaily satirical letters. The first of them appeared on July 21, 1866, the twelfth and last on November 29, 1870. He added to them one other letter and an essay "My Countrymen," from the *Cornhill Magazine* (February, 1866), to make up the book that George Smith, who was his publisher and the editor of both the *Cornhill Magazine* and the *Pall Mall Gazette*, brought out in amusingly appropriate format in February, 1871. The elaborate title was part of the jest: *Friendship's Garland: being the Conversations, Letters, and Opinions of the Late Arminius, Baron Von Thunderten-Tronckh. Collected and edited, with a Dedicatory Letter to Adolescens Leo, Esq., of "The Daily Telegraph," by Matthew Arnold.* The book was bound in white cloth (or, in some copies, a light blue or a medium blue) and funereally bordered in decorous black. Within a small wreath of fourteen gold lilies stamped on the cover was Anchises' tribute to the young Marcellus—*manibus date lilia plenis*—"bestow lilies from full hands."

The brisk and witty *Friendship's Garland* is Arnold's one continuous satire—a fine contribution to the rich and remarkable world of Victorian satirical laughter. Like the topical satire of Pope, it asks the effort of familiarization with its worlds of contemporary allusion to people and to events: Lord Elcho, Lord Stanley, Lord Clanricarde, the Honorable Charles Clifford, Goldwin Smith, Robert Lowe, Frederic Harrison, Edward Miall —"that Israelite," and Hepworth Dixon, the Mormon apologist whose style Arnold defines as "middle-class Macaulayese" and whom Arnold makes sponsor of the regenerating idea of "the great sexual insurrection of the Anglo-Teutonic race." It satirizes the *Star, The Daily Telegraph*, Irish land-reform, compulsory education and the state, social classes, and the controversy about marriage with one's deceased wife's sister.

Arnold also invents his own personae to convey his satire: the Bottles family living at Laburnum House at Reigate; Kitty Crone, a landlady; Zephaniah Diggs, a philoprogenitive poacher; Viscount Lumpington, a "Constitutional Whig"; the Rev. Esau Hittall, "that centaur"—a benighted Tory; Bottles himself, a Radical of the Manchester school. Throughout the letters Arnold assumes the role of the incorrigible, assertive Philistine, while he assigns to his Prussian friend Arminius the eighteenth-century role of the innocent but enlightened foreign visitor. Arminius possesses *Geist*—intelligence and refinement of spirit—("Bismarck would say 'Muzzle them [the Philistines]'; . . . I say, 'Improve them'; but for this time is needed.")²⁹ Towards Arminius, Arnold is Gulliver before the Brobdingnagian king; he is anarchy in the presence of the enlightenment of culture.

The great theme of *Friendship's Garland* in abstract terms is that of *Geist* opposed to *Ungeist*—intelligence opposed to insensibility. It is essentially the dialogue between culture and anarchy expressed exclusively in satirical terms; but *Friendship's Garland* is more condensed in its allusions than is *Culture and Anarchy*, and more oblique because it is more ironic. The fictional anecdotes and the references to fact continuously exemplify failures of reason and of spirit. In the Bottles family are united the prejudices and values of the Philistine concerning industry, individualism, and education. Mr. Bottles's own education at Lycurgus House Academy affords one of the lively sallies in *Friendship's Garland*. Matthew Arnold explains to Arminius with mock enthusiasm:

You are not to suppose from the name of Lycurgus that any Latin and Greek was taught in the establishment; the name only indicates the moral discipline, and the strenuous earnest character, imparted there. As to the instruction, the thoughtful educator who was principal of the Lycurgus House Academy,—Archimedes Silverpump, Ph.D., you must have heard of him in Germany?—had modern views. "We must be men of our age," he used to say. "Useful knowledge, living languages, and the forming of the mind through observation and experiment, these are the fundamental articles of my educational creed." Or, as I have heard his pupil Bottles put it in his expansive moments after dinner . . .: "Original man, Silverpump! fine mind! fine system! None of your antiquated rubbish—all practical work—latest discoveries in science—mind constantly kept excited—lots of interesting experiments —lights of all colours—fizz! fizz! bang! bang! That's what I call forming a man!"³⁰

In the ninth letter, which Arnold addresses directly to the editor of the *Pall Mall Gazette*, Arminius bids farewell to England on the eve of his departure to engage in the Franco-Prussian War. His letter is dated August 9, 1870. Alluding to Matthew Arnold, he sadly remarks to the editor, ". . . he has of late been plunged over head and ears in some dispute of

Greeks of the Lower Empire with your foolish and impracticable Dissenters."[31] In June, 1870, Smith, Elder and Company had published *St. Paul and Protestantism; with an Introduction on Puritanism and the Church of England,* the first of Arnold's series of works attempting "to see things as they really are" in the sphere of changing religious belief.

CHAPTER 7

Geist *and the* Zeitgeist

I *Essays on Religion*

IN retrospect we see the decades of the 1860's and the 1870's, immediately following the publication of Darwin's *The Origin of Species* (1859), as marking the culmination of the crisis of faith in the Victorian era. The crisis was not decisively resolved in the last decades of the century, but it subsided and was diverted in many ways, as in the tentative relativism of Walter Pater or in the cheerless meliorism of Thomas Hardy. Sensitive individuals, such as Carlyle, Tennyson, Clough, and Froude, had recorded their own dilemma earlier in Victoria's reign. But now science aggressively advanced its outposts against orthodoxy, for example, through the continuous lectures and writing of Thomas Henry Huxley and the explosive Belfast address of John Tyndall in 1874. Darwinian methods were applied to social analysis by Sir E. B. Tylor in his *Primitive Culture*. Biology and Anthropology joined Geology and Astronomy as "terrible Muses." To the scepticism of Strauss's *Das Leben Jesu* was added not only the persuasiveness and charm of Renan's *Vie de Jésus* (1863), but the force of *Essays and Reviews* (1860), whose seven learned authors, including Frederick Temple, Mark Pattison, and Benjamin Jowett, were reviled as "Septum Contra Christum" and "the seven extinguishers of the lamps of the Apocalypse."[1]

On a plane often much less intellectual, controversy raged over large issues like that of disestablishment of the Church of England. It expressed itself in laughter at ritualist excesses, or in sectarian feuds like that between the Dean of Ripon and the popular Nonconformist preacher Charles Haddon Spurgeon, or in virulent attacks like that of Charles Kingsley on John Henry Newman, which elicited his *Apologia pro Vita Sua* (1864). The acrimonious temper of the controversy was expressed alike in the unyielding motto of the *Nonconformist*—"The Dissidence of Dissent and the Protestantism of the Protestant Religion"—and in Spurgeon's own motto "Cedo nulli" and in the *Saturday Review*'s attack on Spurgeon as "the Anabaptist Caliban." Moreover, John Morley vigorously proclaimed the Church of England to be "the ally of tyranny, the organ of social oppression, the champion of intellectual bondage."[2]

Against the acrimony of debate, against the claims of those Arnold designated "the friends of science," and against the claims of those he designated "the friends of dogma," Arnold brought the force of his humanism. Having found his mission in the 1860's, he chided Philistine complacency, resistance to ideas, and the wish to do what one likes with appeals for a critical awakening and for a conception of culture as a refining of intellectual and moral sensibilities. In the next decade, he brought the light of his view of culture to bear on the interpretation of religion and the Bible.

St. Paul and Protestantism (1870), *Literature and Dogma* (1873), *God and the Bible* (1875), and *Last Essays on Church and Religion* (1877)—all assembled from periodical essays and lectures written between 1869 and 1876—comprise most of Arnold's writings in this field; they also form a major part of the canon of his prose work. General interest in them has diminished, though not so greatly as in what he had to say about marriage with a deceased wife's sister, or about the Revised Code, or, in his late years, about Irish reform. The faded interest of these issues has tended to isolate in Arnold's work the parts where he is preeminently a literary critic in our contemporary sense of the term, whereas his activity as literary critic was actually an element only, however signal and widely influential, in his embracing concern with the conduct of life. Both Lionel Trilling and Basil Willey seriously consider the religious writings in discussing Arnold's thought, and William Robbins has more recently examined them valuably and without apology in *The Ethical Idealism of Matthew Arnold*. In that study Mr. Robbins handily defines Arnold's reinterpretation of Christianity and the Bible as "an effort to establish their unique claim to permanence as moral and spiritual guides, independent of the discoveries of physical science and the destructive results of historical and rational criticism."[3]

Arnold's *St. Paul and Protestantism* conducts its argument in the "sphere of science." The science that Arnold means is psychology, and he asks us to verify the language of Christianity—of St. Paul in particular—by recognizing not only its poetic or figurative nature but also its "scientific" validity for the psychological experience of each individual. One of Arnold's major premises is that there is in the flux of things a "universal order which the intellect feels after as a law, and the heart feels after as a benefit."[4] A second major premise is that there is a *"stream of tendency by which all things strive to fulfil the law of their being."*[5] He believed that the exaggerated strictness of Calvinism, the sensational element in Methodism, and the anthropomorphism of many denominations arise from the inability of people to understand the metaphorical nature of language and from their own limited sensibility. It is general human experience, not faith, that demonstrates the greater force of Jesus over Socrates: "Socrates inspired boundless friendship and esteem; but the inspiration of reason and conscience is the one inspiration which comes from him, and which impels us to live righteously as he did. A penetrating enthusiasm of love, sympathy, pity, adoration, reinforcing the inspiration of reason and duty, does not belong to Socrates. With Jesus it is different. On this point it is needless to argue; history has proved."[6]

If we can grasp the force of figurative language, Arnold believes that we will be led to understand the symbolic character of "the three cardinal points in Paul's theology"—*dying with Christ, resurrection from the dead, growing into Christ."*[7] Arnold declares "the essential sense in which Paul uses the term *resurrection* is that of a rising, in this visible earthly existence, from the death of obedience to blind selfish impulse, to the life of obedience to the eternal moral order."[8] To the "scientific" validity of Christianity, in this sense, even a naturalist like Goethe can be called as "an unsuspected witness." "Stirb und werde!" he said in the *West-östlicher Divan*: "Die and come to life!"

In Arnold's *Literature and Dogma* the strategy for advancing Christian religion as an aid to culture is to save it from the vulgarizing, popular theology. For Arnold perceived that nineteenth-century popular religion repeated the error of the Hebrews:—"their God came to be a mere magnified and nonnatural man."[9] "Man never knows," Arnold is fond of quoting from Goethe, "how anthropomorphic he is." Anthropomorphism is an element in *Aberglaube*—"extra-belief," to give the word its most neutral translation, or "superstition" to give its most disparaging. *Aberglaube* tends to arise from literalism, from mistaking for material fact the symbolism of poetic language. Even the disciples, in this instance, were fallible hearers of the word and fallible reporters. When Jesus "called himself 'the bread of life' and said, *He that eateth me shall live by me,* they stuck hopelessly fast in the literal meaning of the words."[10]

For Arnold, Jesus's method for bringing about the moral improvements of man is clear, for it is reiterated unmistakably in all four gospels: the consultation of one's own conscience. The message of Jesus, which is contained in the method, is Goethe's "Stirb und werde!": *"He that loveth his life shall lose it, and he that hateth his life in this world shall keep it unto life eternal."*[11]

Reading *Literature and Dogma,* we recall Arnold's comment to his mother in 1865: "No one has a stronger and more abiding sense than I have of the 'daemonic' element—as Goethe calls it —which underlies and encompasses our life."[12] He now devised as a term for God his phrase "the enduring power, not ourselves, that makes for righteousness." He discerned in our appreciation of right conduct "the operation of that mighty *not ourselves* which is in us and around us."[13] The power of Hebraism is in its emphasis on righteousness, but Christianity, with greater sweetness and reasonableness, remains "the greatest and happiest stroke ever yet made for human perfection."

Adverse critical response to *Literature and Dogma* in the *Westminster Review,* the *Quarterly Review,* the *Spectator,* among others, gave Arnold the occasion in *God and the Bible: A Review of Objections to "Literature and Dogma"* to repeat the main points of the two preceding books and to keep current their best phrases. He wished to defend religion from post-Darwinian skepticism as well as from popular Protestantism; he wanted also to defend it from a possible new Deism whose materialistic God "may be best conceived, perhaps, as a kind of tribal God of the Birmingham League. . . . The God of Free Trade, the Free Church, Free Labour, and Free Land."[14] He wanted also to defend it from the bloodless abstraction of metaphysics: "At the mention of that name *metaphysics,* lo, essence, existence, substance, finite and infinite, cause and succession, something and nothing, begin to weave their eternal dance before us! with the confused murmur of their combinations filling all the region governed by *her,* who, far more indisputably than her late-born rival, political economy, has earned the title of the Dismal Science."[15]

The ultimate appeal in *God and the Bible* for the validity of Christianity is experience. Experience verifies that Christianity leads to finer human conduct, the lack of which, for Arnold, precipitated the fall of Greece and now threatens France. Right conduct finds its motive in a heightened sense of joy—"joy and happiness are the magnets to which human life irresistibly moves."[16]

The brilliant young Fellow of Merton College, Francis H. Bradley, turned the light, incandescent even now, of his logical mind upon the questionable grounds for conduct that Arnold proposed and upon his inexpertness in metaphysics. Bradley's attack in *Ethical Studies* (1876) remains an important piece of Arnoldian criticism. Bradley pointed out Arnold's limitations as a logician and his lack of system as a philosopher; he ridiculed Arnold's definition of religion as "poetry touched with emotion" and his definition of God as "the enduring power, not ourselves, which makes for righteousness." In 1887 another Oxford man, William H. Mallock, in *The New Republic,* parodied in the supercilious Mr. Luke, Arnold's effort to separate the literature of Christianity from its dogma. "It is true," Mr. Luke says, "that culture sets aside the larger part of the New Testament as grotesque, barbarous, and immoral; but what remains, purged of its apparent meaning, it discerns to be a treasure beyond all price."[17]

Rationalist though Arnold may appear to be because of his humanistic emphasis and because of the illusion of clarity that his style induces, he was equally a Transcendentalist, at least in his view of historic process. On the one hand, Arnold insists on the superiority of Jesus, among religious teachers, to persuade man to right conduct, and he insists on the responsibility of the individual to strive toward perfection; yet, on the other hand, he believes that collective human experience, seen in the long perspective of time, is itself subject to the plastic stress of a divine mind. In *St. Paul and Protestantism* he says: "Thought and science follow their own law of development, they are slowly elaborated in the growth and forward pressures of humanity, in what Shakespeare calls,—

> the prophetic soul
> Of the wide world dreaming on things to come."[18]

His position at this point is certainly reminiscent of that of Emerson who had written, in his essay on "Montaigne" in *Representative Men* (1850), that, "through the years and centuries, through evil agents, through toys and atoms, a great and beneficent tendency irresistibly streams."[19] Both Emerson and Arnold echo that earlier Transcendentalist, Wordsworth, whose Wanderer in *The Excursion* heard "the mighty stream of tendency" speaking to the meditative mind a message "inaudible/ To the vast multitude."

Despite Arnold's undogmatic theology he wished to preserve the institution of the Church of England. In a lecture at Sion College he defined it as "a great national society for the promotion of what it commonly called *goodness,* and for promoting it through the most effectual means possible, . . . : through the means of the Christian religion and of the Bible."[20] "State Ritualism without theology" is G. K. Chesterton's mocking phrase for Arnold's church. Chesterton believed it was an unconscious restoration of paganism: "Arnold may have thought that he was building an altar to the Unknown God; but he was really building it to Divus Caesar."[21] There seems to be more wit than truth in Chesterton's quip. W. W. Ward more accurately suggested that Arnold's undogmatic theology was in the long run much the same as Herbert Spencer's agnosticism. In our century in his essay, "Arnold and Pater" (1930), T. S. Eliot, who in so many ways is an heir of Arnold, deplored the "degradation of philosophy and religion" begun in these essays on religion; and in *The Use of Poetry and the Use of Criticism,* he compounded disapproval of Arnold's religious thought with dismissal: "In philosophy and theology he was an undergraduate; in religion a Philistine."[22]

H. V. Routh has said of Arnold and of J. A. Froude, "Both of these humanists, like so many other Victorians, wanted to retain the inwardness and vision of older times and yet cultivate a religion which preferred conduct to contemplation."[23] To a reader of Arnold's *Note-Books* the emphasis seems to be equally on contemplation, but the published essays on church and religion support Routh's position.

The development of Arnold's interest from *Culture and Anarchy* to these essays, written with "laborious lucidity"—to use G. K. Chesterton's phrase—is continuous.[24] The essays themselves anticipate a return to literary criticism, with the special emphasis on the ethical that Arnold gave it. If Arnold tended to restrict the modern value of the Bible to its "poetry," he tended in his literary essays to restrict criticism to morality. Virtue and knowledge are interdependent. "The moral and intellectual are always dividing," he quoted from Benjamin Jowett, "yet they must be reunited, and in the highest conception of them are inseparable."[25] He, moreover, set down the proposition, "The noblest races are those which know how to make the most serious use of poetry."[26]

II *The Spirit of the Age*

In his concern with conduct Arnold may appear to make religion synonymous with ethics, and to bring ethics suspiciously close to the discriminating hedonism defined in Walter Pater's famous Conclusion to *The Renaissance*. Discussing the weakening of the force of Christianity from Arnold to Pater to William Butler Yeats, William A. Madden has remarked, "In Arnold's criticism the scale of life's values was already aesthetic, though still emotionally Christian."[27] However, for Arnold the pleasure in goodness arises from obedience to injunctions whose sanctions, revealed in conscience, are supernatural, or, in Arnold's phrasing, are part of the daemonic element that environs us: "He that keepeth the law, happy is he." "It is joy to the just to do judgment."[28] These Proverbs express his sense of the relationship between pleasure and discipline. Pater's hedonistic "stirring of the senses, strange dyes, strange colours" is not an element of Arnold's experience.

The law, the just judgments are expressed through the phenomenon of time. In *Literature and Dogma* Arnold exploited the term *Zeitgeist* to express his apprehension of a daemonic element operating through the flux of time. In so doing, he chose a term, complex in itself, and rich in ambiguities, that has been a source of irritation and confusion to numerous readers and critics. It is a term whose uses direct attention to Arnold's mature philosophical position.

Arnold himself was content to use terms—"the grand style," "stream," "tendency," "the Eternal not ourselves"—as though, in his sometimes Olympian discourse, they had clear definitions and single meanings, leaving the reader to solve the ambiguities; and he was fond of Homer's saying, "wide is the range of words! words may make this way and that." Perhaps if they made "this way," and if by their suggestiveness to the mind and the emotions they lent persuasiveness to the rhetoric, Arnold's end was accomplished; but if they made "that"—as F. H. Bradley devastatingly observed—"we concluded that for us once again the light had shone in darkness."[29] Yet Arnold's intention was not to mislead, although lack of definition avoided commitment. Without pretending to be a philosopher—as he used the term, an originator of ideas—Arnold did put into circulation thoughts and expressions that he created or to which, like "Philistine" or "culture," he gave a special character and currency. The term *Zeitgeist* is among these. It appears frequently in his work; its ambiguities invite scrutiny.

The phenomenon of time, periodicity in history, the doctrine of development, the relation of the individual to the age in which he finds himself and to the age to which he imagines some greater affinity, are interests that are widely reflected in Arnold's writing, as they are a major concern of the Victorian age. They may find expression in metaphors like the "River of Time" or "wave" and "stream" and "tendency," or in more elaborate attempts to establish historic periods, such as epochs of concentration and epochs of expansion in "The Function of Criticism at the Present Time." From Arnold's pessimistic allusion to Goethe's theory of spiral progress in a letter of 1848 to the penultimate entry from Karl Marx in the *Note-Books* for 1888, Arnold displays an interest in the nature of historic process. The names of Hume, Herder, Hegel, Michelet, Renan, to mention only a few, recur in the lists of reading, projected or completed, in his notebooks. Thucydides, Burke, and Niebuhr are referred to as types of the scientific historian. The brief survey of recent political history in Arnold's *England and the Italian Question* and the survey of education in *Schools and Universities on the Continent* are themselves examples of historical writing. Indeed, one modern scholar is persuaded that Arnold's speculations concerning historical process "add up to a philosophy of history so impressive in its comprehensiveness and inner consistency that one wonders that students of Arnold have taken little notice of it."[30]

Although Arnold's interest is widely and variously exhibited, it is neither comprehensive nor consistent. Arnold, who avoided committing himself to systems, although he was anxious to discover first principles, seems to have heeded his father's warning that one should observe "how little any real history is an exact exemplification of abstract principles."[31] The movement of the River of Time in his poem "The Future" reveals an Arnold divided between an idea of happiness conceived in terms of human social progress and an idea of happiness dependent upon intimate relations of the individual with some spiritual origin. The oratorical ending of *A French Eton* (1864) glows with a vision of the ascent of "the arduous ladder whereby man climbs toward his perfection"; but Arnold and the Scholar-Gipsy of "Thyrsis" (1866) tentatively and in solitude seek "a fugitive and gracious light." And the essays of Arnold's final decade suggest a diminished interest in historical process and causation. Yet Arnold's Time-Spirit is an evidence of his interest in the phenomenon of change.

The term *Zeitgeist* first appears in a letter of July 20, 1848. "My dear Clough," Arnold wrote, with his characteristic air of negligence in reference, "Goethe says somewhere that the Zeitgeist when he was young caused everyone to adopt the Wolfian theories about Homer, himself included: and that when he was in middle age the same Zeitgeist caused them to leave these theories for the hypothesis of one poem and one author: inferring that in these matters there is no certainty, but alternating dispositions." Here *Zeitgeist* appears to mean current opinion, current intellectual fashion. The spirit itself operates, with a certain whimsicality, in the realm of opinion. It is as if to say with Olivia's fool, "And thus the whirligig of time brings in his revenges." The implication is that Arnold can elect to avoid the pressure of local opinion, that he can find stability beyond the flux of fashion. *Zeitgeist* is an emblem of instability, but "whirligig" is far removed from the metaphysics of universal history.

Arnold introduces the *Zeitgeist* in conjunction with Goethe's name, but he may equally well have met the word and found his early meaning for it in Carlyle, who had employed it in "Characteristics" (1831) and in *Sartor Resartus* (1833-34). Carlylean vehemence stirred Arnold when he next introduced the word in a letter to Clough in November, 1848. For 1848 is still within the period of Arnold's admiration for Carlyle, although Arnold labeled him a "moral desperado" in the fall of 1849. In March, 1848, he sent his mother Carlyle's foaming article on Louis Philippe from the *Examiner*, with his own final comment "How deeply restful it comes upon one, amidst the hot dizzy trash one reads about these changes everywhere. . . . The source of repose in Carlyle's article is that he alone puts aside the din and whirl and brutality which envelop a movement of the masses to fix his thought on its ideal invisible character."[32]

More important, however, than the Carlylean vehemence of expression in the letter to Clough are the Carlylean ideas that Arnold reinforced in the final clause: that the *Zeitgeist* is escapable, therefore local and temporary, and that it embodies transitory as against absolute values. Arnold writes:

I have been at Oxford the last two days and hearing Sellar and the rest of that clique, who know neither life nor themselves, rave about your poem gave me a strong almost bitter feeling with respect to them, the age, the poem, even you. Yes I said to myself something tells me I can, if need be, at last dispense with them all, even with him: better that, than be sucked for an hour even into the Time Stream in which they and he plunge and bellow. I became calm in spirit, but uncompromising, almost stern. More English than European, I said finally, more American than English: and took up Obermann, and refuged myself with him in his forest against your Zeit Geist.[33]

The age, the Time Stream, the *Zeitgeist* are here interrelated. The *Zeitgeist* has meaning in the neutral sense of the spirit or temper of the age; it also has meaning in a sense more metaphysical than definition as "the thought or feeling of a period or of an age" would imply. It is the character of the age, especially if one views that age as expressive of a process at odds with eternal values.

The connotation of *Zeitgeist* in the letters to Clough is to be understood not in the context only of a letter, but of *the* letters; for the reiterated complaints of "unpoetical," of the "damned times," of the lack of nourishment, of the blankness and barrenness, of the aridity of the age, constitute the character the Geist embodies. Allied with the image of the Charybdean Time Stream, it suggests more than this embodiment. The voracious Time Stream is the continuous process that subsumes the spirit of any particular time; against its surging if fruitless activity is the aloof and permanent, though sad, spiritual repose signified by Obermann's forest. That one's age is in some measure escapable, that the artist may preserve his integrity by turning "deeper in the bowering wood!/ Averse, as Dido did, with gesture stern," in pursuit of universal values are ideas that Carlyle, like Arnold, applauded.

The pattern of Arnold's thought becomes clearer if it is compared with Carlyle's. Carlyle, puzzled by the phenomenon of time, tended to regard it as illusory; or, if he admitted it to the "quite undue rank of Realities," he thought of it as a force of negation to be overcome, like the dull dense mass on which Shelley's "plastic stress" operates; or, like Goethe's Mephistopheles, a spirit that denies. He ponders in *Sartor Resartus*: "Often have I fancied how, in thy hard life-battle, thou wert shot at, and slung at, wounded, hand-fettered, hamstrung, browbeaten and bedevilled by the Time-Spirit (*Zeitgeist*) in thyself and other, till the good soul first given thee was seared into grim rage; and thou hadst nothing for it but to leave in me an indignant appeal to the Future, and living speaking Protest against the Devil, as that same Spirit not of the Time only, but of Time itself, is well named!"[34] Arnold, on the other hand, does not seem to have been perplexed, except in the poem "In Utrumque Paratus," by the possible ideality of his universe;

but he was fully persuaded of the arid, dispiriting nature of his own day, and of his obligation to fasten on absolute ethical values, ascertainable through self-knowledge, fixed above the flux.

In the letters to Clough, the *Zeitgeist* expresses for Arnold a force to be abhorred, local, negative. On the other hand, a decade later, in his review "Dr. Stanley's Lectures on the Jewish Church" (1863), the term commands respect; it begins to emerge as the agent of necessary change in the realm of intellect, a role that is established more firmly in *St. Paul and Protestantism* and yet more insistently and triumphantly asserted, for at least rhetorical ends, to strengthen Arnold's case in *Literature and Dogma*. The term that in 1848 expressed the dullness of the world to be overcome expresses in the 1860's the plastic stress itself.

Approximately a decade also separates the melancholy conclusion to Arnold's view of progress in "The Future"—"But what was before us we know not,/ And we know not what shall succeed"—and that glowingly hopeful prospect in *A French Eton* of a later generation "mounting some new step in the arduous ladder whereby man climbs toward his perfection." Even in the earlier years of Arnold's maturity there exist evidences of his changing historical awareness; if we cannot say categorically who shaped his thinking, or precisely when or in what way, we can yet discern influences and receptive attitudes that may well account for the strong modifying of the early pessimism, either because they suggested new modes of thinking or confirmed ideas he was himself working out.

Among the earlier poems not only "The Future," but also "Revolutions" (1852) and the ironic "Progress" (1852) reflect an interest in historic process, dilemmas that must be resolved, and unyielding tenets with which Arnold had to reconcile any philosophy of change. "Revolutions" proposes that civilizations —Greece, Rome, England, France—have been the inadequate, and not the final, efforts of man to express a divine order, one which exists in the mind of God, but which man is capable of realizing. "Progress" balances man's desire for the new dispensation in primitive Christian and modern times; and, belying what expectations the title might arouse of materialistic meaning, the work

concludes with the admonition *"Thou must be born again!"* The
individualism which insists on man's creativity; the authority of
conscience, which is the private and intuitive consciousness of
a divine moral order; and the premise of individual moral regeneration as the condition of "progress" are Arnold's fundamental concerns—and they are implicit here. They constitute the
"bedrock *credo*," prior to any philosophy of history.[35]

These tenets are always supportable in the exclusive privacy
of Obermann's forest; Arnold's problem was to find a reading of
the history of humanity in society that could contain them, for
his growing sense of public responsibility compelled him to
accomodate a larger experience than that of the individual. Ideas
about periodicity in history and about the role of Providence,
ideas conceiving history as Revelation, and ideas concerning the
nature of development were available to him in writings by men
who interested him by the early 1850's. Edmund Burke's fragmentary *Essay towards an Abridgment of the English History*
combined rationalistic objectivity in narration with the admission
of a providential ordering of change. Carlyle's eclecticism may
well have provided Arnold with insight into the concept of revelation through history favored among the German Transcendental-
ists. B. G. Niebuhr displayed a scientific method and asserted the
action of Providence in events. C. K. J. Bunsen, the friend of
Arnold's father, justified alteration in church matters as "development," and his " 'God in history' is," as one of Arnold's
early reviewers noted, "Arnold's God in human experience."[36]
John Henry Newman, whom Arnold had heard with interest at
Oxford, and from whom he acknowledged having "learnt habits,
methods, ruling ideas," formulated a theory of development.
And Dr. Thomas Arnold's reading of divine and moral process
in history was one of many intellectual heritages for his son.[37]

III   *The Plastic Stress*

Disliking metaphysical abstractions, yet compelled to express
his reflections on historic process, Arnold employed the persuasiveness, perhaps the evasiveness, of symbol. *Zeitgeist* appears
to have offered for a time a needed measure of potency and
elusiveness. In a period when his agnosticism was waning, it

afforded a device for intimating, without definite commitment, the concern of an intelligent, moral force in human activity.

In his essay on Doctor Stanley's *Lectures* Arnold distinguished between a world of purely intellectual life, which a few men— Parmenides, Spinoza, Hegel are his examples—inhabit, and the world of religious life, where strong feelings attach to certain fixed ethical ideas. The values of the latter world are absolute; the values of the former, operant in the areas of philosophy, science, letters, are mutable, though they are not mutable in a frivolous way. They accord with what fascinated Arnold, a doctrine of development. "Intellectual ideas," he writes, "are not the essence of the religious life; still the religious life connects itself, as I have said, with certain intellectual ideas, and all intellectual ideas follow a development independent of the religious life."[38]

The term *Zeitgeist* gave Arnold a symbol to express mutability at the same time that it suggested an extramundane force ordering the change in accordance with some law. It is difficult to perceive what form this law takes for Arnold except that reasonableness, that is, rationality, seems to increase in time, both in areas of enlightenment and in the numbers of persons enlightened; but with reference to infallible moral law Arnold would agree that like the law invoked by Sophocles' Antigone, it does not have its origin today or yesterday, but is from all time.

As in the case of Arnold's initial reference to the *Zeitgeist* in the letters to Clough, Goethe is paraphrased to provide orientation for the word; but, whereas the *Zeitgeist* is there reported to have caused opinion to veer from hypothesis of single to that of multiple authorship of the Homeric poems between Goethe's youth and middle age, it now moves with less undignified haste, taking a lifetime to effect the change. "Goethe somewhere remarks," says Arnold again, as he sympathizes with the intellectually awake yet pious clergyman in a time of rapidly increasing information, "how the *Zeit-Geist*, as he calls it, the *Time-Spirit*, irresistibly changes the ideas current in the world. When he was young, he says, the Time-Spirit had made every one disbelieve in the existence of a single Homer: when he was old, it was bearing every one to a belief in it."[39] How such fluctuation of opinion as this about single or multiple authorship illustrates the world of intellectual development in which Parmenides,

Spinoza, and Hegel live is not clear. Yet Arnold has introduced a useful rhetorical term, and he continues immediately: "Intellectual ideas, which the majority of men take from the age in which they live, are the dominion of this Time-Spirit; not moral and spiritual life, which is original in each individual."

Arnold could hardly have believed that ideas about authorship and philosophical ideas are of the same category, that Time-Spirit is here really used synonymously. Here his strategy was to adduce, from one context, the authority lent by Goethe's name to witness, in another context, the pressure of a metaphysical force shaping the "development" of ecclesiastical thought. The *Zeitgeist* is not now a force against which the artist must "refuge" himself. It has more validity than mere opinion. The majority are not reprehensible for taking their intellectual ideas from their age, for these ideas are under a "dominion" not their own; they are "liable to development and change." The spirit operates, we are told, "irresistibly," outside the sphere of moral and religious ideas. Thus the Articles of the Church of England, reflecting the ideas of the English Reformers and the Reformation, deserve review. "Insensibly the Time-Spirit brings to men's minds a consciousness that certain of these ideas have undergone such development, such change."[40]

Arnold, who so habitually emphasized the role of the individual in the world of thought, may in this essay seem to make him an instrumentality in a dialectical process. The greatness of the great religious reformer, he says at the beginning of the essay, "does not consist in his having these new ideas (that is, intellectual ideas), in originating them. The ideas are in the world; they come originally from the sphere of pure thought; they are put into circulation by the spirit of the time. The greatness of a religious reformer consists in his reconciling them with their religious life, in his starting this life upon a fresh period in company with them." The passage is ambiguous at a critical point. What does Arnold mean by "the sphere of pure thought"? How do ideas "come" into the world? Does to "put into circulation" mean "to initiate" or "to stimulate"? Does the phrase "by the spirit of the time" mean by a transcendental force, or by the favorable state of popular knowledge at a given time?

A study of "Matthew Arnold the Epistemologist" has not been

written; and the context of these phrases does not answer all the questions. The above passage from "Dr. Stanley's Lectures on The Jewish Church" is to be understood by the needs of his rhetoric and in the light of the role Arnold may have imagined for himself. Soon to attempt a career of religious reformer, he disclaims originality as a thinker; he sets up a category of "philosophers" to account for novelty in thought; and he confines the role of religious thinker to the reinterpretation of the religious life in accordance with the current rationalistic intellectual ideas.

The danger of constructing an epistemology or a rigid philosophy of history out of his metaphors is indicated by Arnold himself in the first essay on St. Paul and Protestantism when he says of St. Paul's use of figurative language: "He uses within the sphere of religious emotion expressions which, in this sphere, have an eloquence and a propriety, but which are not to be taken out of it and made into formal scientific propositions."[41] Arnold's warning reinforces the probability that the more limited meaning of the "spirit of the time" is nearer to his intention. But, when he subsequently introduced into the essay on Stanley's *Lectures* the idea of a more dramatic *Zeitgeist*, operating "irresistibly" and "insensibly" on men's consciousness in accordance with a doctrine of development, he emphasized the latent ontological implications, and heightened the anthropomorphic ones; and he found a metaphorical ally to reinforce the argument in his first two books of religious controversy. "Man never knows how anthropomorphic he is," Arnold repeats after Goethe in *Literature and Dogma*.

The tendency of critics and historians of Christian doctrine—Renan, Reuss, Baur, Strauss—with whom Arnold became increasingly familiar in the decade of the 1860's—and collaterally with the preparation of the major works of religious controversy—confirmed not only his own conviction that the importance of Christianity is in relation to human conduct, but also the optimism inherent in the concept of development in human enlightenment. Renan's conviction, expressed in *L'Avenir de la science,* that amid its oscillations humanity tends through increasing rationality towards perfection, finds its echo in Arnold's *A French Eton.* Renan's opinion, "Le temps me semble de plus en plus le facteur universel, le grand coefficient de l'éternel 'devenir,'" was profoundly congenial to Arnold. ("More and more time seems to me the universal agent, the great coefficient of eternal becoming.") Arnold shared the belief of Émile de Laveleye that the change in religious thought was "une évolution de doctrines tout intérieure, qui, par le travail lent, continu, sans passions and sans bruit, de l'érudition, tend à modifier les traditions, les croyances, et en dernier résultat à éliminer le surnaturel."[42] ("An internal evolution in beliefs which, by the silent, continuous, passionless and noiseless work of knowledge tends to modify traditions and beliefs, and ultimately to do away with the supernatural.") His own religious essays attempted to demonstrate the validity of such a position.

In "Puritanism and the Church of England," Arnold declares his doctrine of development, quoting Newman for its formulation:

A historic Church cannot choose but allow the principle of development, for it is written in its institutions and history. An admirable writer, in a book which is one of his least known works, but which contains, perhaps, even a greater number of profound and valuable ideas than any other one of them, has set forth, both persuasively and truly, the impression of this sort which Church-history cannot but convey. "We have to account," says Dr. Newman, in his *Essay on Development*, "for that apparent variation and growth of doctrine which embarrasses us when we would consult history for the true idea of Christianity. The increase and expansion of the Christian creed and ritual, and the variations which have attended the process in the case of individual writers and churches, are the necessary attendants on any philosophy or polity which takes possession of the intellect and heart, and has had any wide or extended dominion. From the nature of the human mind, time is necessary for full comprehension and perfection of great ideas."[43]

A "principle of development," or a "law of development," is, as we have seen, a premise of Arnold's contention that the special tenets of Puritan dogma are intolerable foundations for Christian faith. And it is also a contention that, although Hooker and Butler and Newman have perceived that "the whole Bible is written on the principle of development," the church has not yet provided an adequate vehicle for the interpretation and accommodation of current developments of thought and science. Moreover, the Catholic Church has "vainly imagined herself to have had the power to produce" the right philosophical developments. What agency then does forward our ideas? Arnold's answer is that "their ripeness and unripeness, as Dr. Newman most truly says, are not an effect of our wishing or resolving. Rather do they seem brought about by a power such as Goethe figures by the *Zeit-Geist* or Time-Spirit, and St. Paul describes as a divine power *revealing* additions to what we possess already."[44] Not only is the *Zeitgeist* here a different force from the abhorrent pressure of contemporaneity against which Arnold wished to "refuge" himself in 1848; it is more daemonic than Goethe's figure, or even than the *Zeitgeist* of the review of Dr. Stanley's *Lectures*. Its operation, if vague in mode, is admittedly divine; time as historic process has ontological meaning.

Yet we must qualify the representation of such a conception as a positive tenet in Arnold's creed by his own two reservations, "such as" and "do seem." Like the Demon, Ghost, and Heaven of Shelley's "Hymn to Intellectual Beauty," the *Zeitgeist* is the record of an endeavor to express in words a process that the heart of mankind apprehends; like the grounds of Wordsworth's intimations of immortality, it may be "too shadowy a notion to be recommended to faith." But the force with which the reservations are stated seems minor compared to the potency of the rhetorical figure.

Arnold's preface to *St. Paul and Protestantism* introduces the image as a serious ground of the argument. "In the second place," he says, "the version we propound of St. Paul's line of thought is not new, is not of our discovering. It belongs to the 'Zeit-Geist,' or *time-spirit*, it is in the air, and many have long been anticipating it, preparing it, setting forth this and that part of it, till there is not a part, probably, of all we have said, which has not already been said by others before us, and said more learnedly and fully than we can say it."[45]

The term may here be taken only to suggest what is widely current, what is characteristic of the temper of the age; and the force of persuasion in the passage is again in part the modesty which Arnold's metaphor allows him. But, within a few sentences, the potentialities of the term for being anthropomorphic are realized. Its capacity to suggest a cosmic force was no doubt one of Arnold's devices for persuasion, a device more powerful

than the enumeration he could have made of the easily discoverable names of those who constituted for him the con-
sensus of informed opinion in this area. The figure also served
adequately to suggest a philosophic belief about human history
that Arnold inclined to favor, but which he declined to assert
in terms of any more binding philosophical proposition.

Continuing, Arnold says, the Hebraisers "have little notion
of letting their consciousness play on things freely, little ear
for the voice of the 'Zeit-Geist.'" Within a few more sentences
the term is associated with the compulsion of a principle of
change. Arnold's reading of St. Paul is presented, climactically,
as a "product of nature," as a "fruit of sound development, a
genuine product of the 'Zeit-Geist.'" None of this accumulated
force is lost when the figure reappears as an agency in the
destruction of tenets of Calvinistic Puritanism: "The predesti-
narian and solifidian dogmas, for the very sake of which our
Puritan churches came into existence, begin to feel the irresistible
breath of the 'Zeit-Geist'; some of them melt quicker, others
slower, but all of them are doomed."

These passages define the function of the *Zeitgeist* in the argument conducted in *St. Paul and Protestantism;* the final appearance, however, introduces a formula that confirms the belief that
Arnold wished to suggest a cosmic power, operating through
historic intellectual process, when he used the term, at least in
this passage and in *Literature and Dogma.* The *Zeitgeist* and
some rationalistic element are now compounded in a phrase that
by repitition becomes a formula. Thus in *St. Paul and Protestantism,* he admits, it was natural that the Puritans should deter-
minedly resist assaults on the doctrines of predestination or justi-
fication at a time when they believed that such doctrines
constituted the essence of Christianity. "That is why," he continues, "when the 'Zeit-Geist' and the general movement of
men's religious ideas is beginning to reveal that the Puritan gospel
is not the essence of Christianity, we have been desirous to spread
this revelation to the best of our power, and by all the aids of
plain popular exposition to help it forward."[46]

The best orientation to Arnold's meaning of *Zeitgeist* is provided by the premise he invites the sympathetic reader to grant
him in his preface. He obliquely reaffirms his perception that

development is a law of history—the history not only of states but, as the book ultimately discloses, of the human mind. Arnold is content to apprehend Divinity as process, without other additional personal testimony than individual consciousness. Ironically placing himself in the category of traditional believer, he makes the important statement:

It is because we cannot trace God in history that we stay the craving of our minds with a fancy-account of him, made up by putting scattered expressions of the *Bible* together, and taking them literally; it is because we have a scanty sense of the life of humanity, that we proceed in the like manner in our scheme of a future state. He that cannot watch the God of the *Bible,* and the salvation of the *Bible,* gradually and on an immense scale discovering themselves and *becoming,* will insist on seeing them ready-made.[47]

The stature of Bishop Hooker, who Arnold claims had a historic sense, who assigned reason as the sole criterion of judgment for deducing dogma from Scripture—the stature of Hooker is to be measured by his grasp of the role of development in the history of human intelligence. Surely apprehension of this concept is enough, Arnold cries, "without our expecting him to say that the Church-dogmas of his time, the dogma of the Athanasian Creed among the rest, which were not seriously in question yet, on which the Time-Spirit, had not then turned his light, were *false developments.*" The life of humanity appears to grow, on the side of intellect, as more and more areas of belief are validated, or rejected, by reason. Divinity manifests itself in so far as this process is discernible.

The Time-Spirit is a name for divinity thus manifesting itself, not through its other channel, conscience, but through the history of the human mind. So considered, Arnold's mocking (and perhaps uncomprehending) reference at the close of the preface to Pope Pius IX, who had so recently as July, 1870, proclaimed the dogma of papal infallibility, gains point, as it may also suggest confirmation of Arnold's meaning. For the surprise is not only at the arrogance of "that amiable old pessimist" arrogating to himself infallibility, but at the assumption that the discovery of truth is a power of individuals rather than of historic process.

Examination of Arnold's meanings for *Zeitgeist* is not equivalent to an examination of his reading of history, but it is a component of an understanding of that reading. So regarded, Arnold's use of the word should not be dismissed as a fetish, although something of the impatience that such criticism reflects arises from Arnold's unformulated and undefined use. Yet to have expressed the formula that would have contained and defined *Zeitgeist* would have been to propose a dogma concerning the nature of history that Arnold would have declined very often or very long to accept. To rest with no formulation more rigid than metaphor was to suggest a *seeming* nature in historic process that was a sufficient commitment.

Arnold's writing does not express a consistent view of history, nor does he ever arrive at what for him constituted certainty about the dynamics of history. He published in 1861, and reprinted in 1879, a statement expressing two attitudes at odds with full belief in a deterministic process in history. He said, speaking of moral perfection as conceived by Christian ethics, "Human thought, which made all institutions, inevitably saps them, resting only in that which is absolute and eternal."[48] The conviction that human thought originates with human beings and makes and remakes temporal institutions implies an individualism incompatible with pure determinism.

The latitude that Arnold's mind exhibited for entertaining opposed possibilities is dramatically shown in the last entries in his *Note-Books* where the determinism of Karl Marx ("Society is a sort of organism on the growth of which conscious efforts can exercise little effect") and the individualism of Thomas à Kempis ("If there be joy in the world, surely a man of pure heart possesseth it") are juxtaposed. Social determinism and religious individualism are opposed possibilities unless we admit the romantic dichotomy with which Arnold began his poetic career and sequester ourselves from the uncontrollable phenomenal world in Obermann's forest of the isolated spirit.

The almost complete absence of the *Zeitgeist* from *God and the Bible*, Arnold's reply to objections to *Literature and Dogma*, might well caution us against suggesting that it was a necessary term in expressing his philosophy of history; and indeed we should guard against assuming that each appearance of the term is necessarily the reassertion of Arnold's belief. The figure was useful in the rhetoric of persuasion; it could incline the mind to belief in some kind of spiritual force causing men to hold certain opinions; yet, by remaining metaphorical, it was not open to such specific rebuttal as would have been an abstract formulation, which Arnold was unwilling, and possibly unable, to make.

How little necessary to his interpretation of intellectual change was such a concept as that embodied in this metaphor, is perhaps indicated by his being able to survey changes, for example in the canon of the Bible, over centuries without invoking its instrumentality. On the other hand, how potent its pressure in behalf of the argument might be, if only from its suggestiveness, is indicated by Arnold's choosing to place it in the title of the pair of discourses, "Bishop Butler and the Zeit-Geist," while almost entirely omitting to refer to it in the body of the writing.

The issues of time and change, however, are not absent from either of these two essays, nor from "A Psychological Parallel" in *Last Essays on Church and Religion*. Although the issues of time and change are not absent, there is a diminished effort to suggest a theory, however shadowy, of causation. In the discourses on Bishop Butler we hear, with reference to intellectual changes, that "the time inevitably arrives" when in their widening experience men question the authorities of their youth; we hear that "there are moments when" certain subjects are unpopular; we hear, with more resounding and apocalyptic rhetoric, that "the time comes,—sooner or later the time comes,— to individuals and even to societies, when the foundations of the great deep are broken up, and everything is in question"; but of causation or design we learn nothing. The figure *Zeit-geist* is cited once in the first lecture. There its use is purely rhetorical. It signifies nothing more than human reason. The figure is cited once in the second lecture; the function and meaning are the same.

Butler's *Analogy of Religion*, Arnold concludes, has failed our matured experience of human psychology: "It seemed once to have a spell and a power; but the *Zeit-Geist* breathes upon it, and we rub our eyes and it has the spell and the power no longer."[49] Human reason has dissipated the error. The drift of these discourses insists on a strictly empirical basis for all man's knowledge; in that effort, metaphysical speculation, however limited, has no place. Even the doctrine of development to which Arnold seemed committed has shrunk almost to an Aristotelian principle of potentiality for individual growth, although Arnold does admit the growth of social behavior out of experience in society. "For men are solidary, or co-partners, and not isolated."

In summary, the term *Zeitgeist,* as Arnold uses it, requires constant reexamination and redefinition as it appears from instance to instance; and the meaning is related to the strategy of the argumentation as well as to the thought of the passage. In the letters to Clough, *Zeitgeist* means the current fashionable opinion, especially as opposed to ascertainable critical absolutes. And, in the period of Arnold's greatest interest in intellectual change, especially as manifested by new interpretations of Christian doctrine, the figure of the *Zeitgeist* signifies a cosmic spiritual power that wills the development of human reason and that reveals development in the sequence of historic time. In Arnold's essays on religion the expression had its special usefulness both as a rhetorical device connoting a supernatural agency that favored Arnold's views, and as a means of suggesting, without dogmatic assertion, the probability that the wisdom of man is ultimately the wisdom of God.

CHAPTER 8

"Skies of Brass and Iron"

I *The Return to Literary Criticism*

ARNOLD'S solitary wanderer in "A Summer Night" protested
sadly against the sterile routine of ordinary human existence:

> For most men in a brazen prison live,
> Where, in the sun's hot eye,
> With heads bent o'er their toil, they languidly
> Their lives to some unmeaning taskwork give.

He likewise deplored the futility of inevitable shipwreck in
Byronic revolt—for the individual will is curbed by necessity
in the form of moral imperatives. But he found in the remote
yet clear transparency of moonlight and stars an emblem of the
human spirit, alone in its individuality, constant in its activity,
and vast in its capability.

A note of wistful aspiration imbues Arnold's poems of the
1850's with a characteristic melancholy; in the 1870's and 1880's
the operations of the *Zeitgeist* and the stream of tendency
with an equally characteristic optimism color the encouraging
and admonishing voice that addressed the English and the
American public on a multiplicity of subjects—social, educational, political, literary—through the media of lectures, book
reviews, and essays for the periodical press. In 1864 Arnold wrote
to Richard Cobden that he discerned in the new generation of
the middle class an increased accessibility of spirit. In his notebook for 1878 Arnold entered the comment of Condorcet in his
Vie de M. Turgot: "L'ordre naturel tend à rendre l'opinion
générale de plus en plus conforme à la verité." ("The natural
order of things tends to bring general opinion increasingly in

conformity with truth.") Arnold must have taken pleasure in such confirmation of his basic hopefulness for the transformation of "that wonderful creature, the British Philistine," and of his American counterpart, both living under skies of "brass and iron," both perplexed in "mazes of heat and sound."

The transformation, however much aided by tendency, does not have for Arnold the easy, if slow, inevitableness of Godwinian prefectibility; it depends, instead, on the tireless effort of the individual to acquire culture. Whatever outward manifestations culture may have in the language and ceremony of the Anglican service, or in the manners of the British aristocracy, or, reading Arnold's letters we might almost say, in the amenities of tea and croquet with the Rothschilds at Aston Clinton, the transformation is essentially an inward matter. "Except a man be born *from above*," Arnold reiterated, "he cannot have part in the society of the future."[1] The transformation also requires persistent endeavor in conveying to the public an idea of humanistic individual culture.

In the later essays Arnold repeatedly defines civilization as "the humanisation of man in society." The aim of humanization lends a unifying element to the widely diverse essays that Arnold chose to make up two more books, *Mixed Essays* (1879) and *Irish Essays and Others* (1882), before he undertook what he amusedly called his "invasion of America."[2] For the former of these books, Arnold at one point proposed the title *Literature and Civilisation—Mixed Essays.*[3] He pointed out to George Smith, his publisher, who had recently reported to him disappointing sales for *Last Essays on Church and Religion,* that the *Mixed Essays* might be helped by its having "a good deal of literature in it."

Mixed Essays does mark, in a limited way, a return to the business of literary criticism, with "A Guide to English Literature," "George Sand," and two essays on Edmond Scherer, "A French Critic on Milton," and "A French Critic on Goethe." Literary criticism for Arnold is always in a large measure pragmatic, to use Meyer Abrams' helpful term in *The Mirror and the Lamp.* Literature is indisputably, Arnold says, "a powerful agency for benefiting the world and for civilising it."[4] It is an agency in developing the four inclusive powers that he now identifies as building civilization: "the power of conduct, the power of intellect and knowledge, the power of beauty, and the power of social life and manners."[5] Among these powers intellect and knowledge would appear to have most to do with the disinterestedness—"to see the object as in itself it really is"— that remains a constant principle in his literary criticism.

This objectivity enables the critic to discriminate among poets —as Victor Hugo could not discriminate among Homer, Dante, Corneille, Voltaire—or to perceive that *Faust* may not be what Hermann Grimm asserted it to be, "the greatest work of the greatest poet of all times and of all peoples." This detachment enables even an Englishman to prefer Scherer's reserved judgment about Milton to Macaulay's "metallic" rhetorical enthusiasm. It enables even a German to laugh at the sentimentality of Herder's fiancée, who wrote him " 'that one night in the depth of the woods she fell on her knees as she looked at the moon, and that having found some glow worms she put them into her hair, being careful to arrange them in couples that she might not disturb their loves.' "[6]

The culture recommended for the individual in these essays is not essentially different from that recommended in *Culture and Anarchy*. The concern for "the power of social life and manners" and for "the power of beauty," however, puts into focus external amenities, on the one hand, and, on the other, esthetic considerations that introduce a fresh element in Arnold's literary criticism.

In "Equality," which was first published in the *Fortnightly Review* in March, 1878, Arnold praises France for its *"esprit de société,"* for having achieved a "high and charming ideal of social intercourse and manners," which it has communicated to its middle class through social equality. On the other hand, he says, "In America, perhaps, we see the disadvantages of having social equality before there has been any such high standard of social life and manners formed."[7] Arnold was pleased with Cardinal Giacomo Antonelli's pointing out to him, when he visited schools in Italy, that even illiterate Romans habitually judged in terms of an awareness of beauty—"è brutto," "è bello."[8] The limitations of England's middle class and lower class are discernible now not only in their tendency to Hebraise, but in their tendency to be "gay or rowdy," as exemplified for Arnold in the war fever expressed by G. W. Hunt's popular music-hall song of 1878: "We don't want to fight, but, by jingo, if we do,/ We've got the ships, we've got the men, and we've got the money too."

Arnold writes more explicitly of "the power of beauty" in these years near the turn of the decade. His essays on Wordsworth, Keats, Byron, and on "The Study of Poetry" were written between 1879 and 1881. He entered in his notebook for 1880 a remark of Sidney Colvin, then Slade Professor of Fine Arts at Cambridge: "Poetry does not illuminate life by helping us to examine and judge, so much as by helping us to feel and be. What we owe to poetry is not powers of analysis sharpened and of judgment fortified, but imagination nourished and enriched."[9] A few pages later there is a series of propositions from Frederick Leighton's address of December 10, 1879, to the students of the Royal Academy, in which he said: "It is in its power to excite certain sides of our aesthetic sensibility, and not in its power of imitation that the strength of Art lies"; and again, "In the emotion aroused by the phenomena of life, the central and culminating fact is our interest in man."[10]

Almost immediately after this entry, Arnold set down this thought from Walter Pater's essay on Wordsworth (1874): "To witness with appropriate emotions the spectacle afforded by men and nature is the aim of all culture." We wonder in reading these entries if Arnold might have recalled as he made them his comment about the early death of his father: "The interest of the world and of the spectacle of its events as they unroll themselves is what I regret for him; indeed, this is the main part of what is valuable in life for anybody."[11] But the context of that comment clearly does not suggest the Epicurean savoring of experiences implicit in Pater and Leighton, although it is not entirely absent from Arnold's talk about "high beauty" and "tact" in "The Study of Poetry."

In the 1870's the writings of Walter Pater and John Addington Symonds, the manifold activities in literature and decorative design of William Morris, and the vogue of Burne-Jones at the Grosvenor Gallery for a few years after 1877 gave background enough for satire of the new estheticism to be popularly meaningful. For example, George Du Maurier laughed at it through his sketches in *Punch* in 1880 and Gilbert and Sullivan in their *Patience* of 1881. Clearly the changing atmosphere to which Arnold's own view of culture had contributed was not lost on him, for he wrote March 25, 1881, to his friend Ernest Fontanès, ". . . man feels himself to be a more various and richly endowed animal than the old religious theory of human life allowed, and he is endeavouring to give satisfaction to the long suppressed and still imperfectly understood instincts of this varied nature. I think this revolution is happening everywhere."[12] Arnold discerned in the relaxation of strictness, sombreness, narrowness in the English religious world an "awakening demand for beauty"; and he said, "I think it is, like all inevitable revolutions, a salutary one, but it greatly requires watching and guiding." Arnold shared the confidence of his father who had long before affirmed that ". . . the tendency of society is to become more and more liberal."[13]

Arnold made time in the midst of daily school inspection for an edition of *The Six Chief Lives from Johnson's "Lives of the Poets"* (1878); for selections from Wordsworth (1879) and Byron (1881), with critical prefaces, in Macmillan's recently launched Golden Treasury Series of classics; for an important introduction, now known as "The Study of Poetry," to T. H. Ward's *The English Poets* (1880); and for a collection of *Letters, Speeches and Tracts on Irish Affairs by Edmund Burke* (1881). The first four of these works reflect Arnold's reviving interest in his role as a man of letters; the last of them was related directly to his role as a social and political guide. For Burke provided, he thought, a guide on the side of moderation and reasonableness to heal the breach between England and Ireland. And Burke had also warned, as Arnold warned continuously in more contemporary terms, against denial of Irish demands: "If men are kept as being no better than half citizens for any length of time, they will be made whole Jacobins."[14]

II *The American Lecture Tour*

On September 30, 1882, Lord Derby presented Arnold to an audience in St. George's Hall at the inauguration of the new autumn term of University College, Liverpool. Ironically and with an air of negligence Arnold admitted to a possible characterization of himself as "a nearly worn-out man of letters, with one nostrum for practical application, his nostrum of public schools for the middle classes; and with a frippery of phrases about sweetness and light, seeing things as they really are, knowing the best that has been thought and said in the world, which never had very much solid meaning, and have now quite lost the gloss and charm of novelty."[15]

The mocking characterization assumes what was, of course, the fact; Arnold had created, by the age of fifty-nine, a well-established public image. The image reveals three concurrent and inter-related concerns—those of social reformer, moralist, and critic. Confessing his own repetitiousness, he used new phrases in the Liverpool Address to develop some of his favorite themes. The old antithesis of Hebraism and Hellenism is replaced by one between Luther and Voltaire. "Seeing things as they really are" is allied with the scientific spirit of the occasion (the opening of the School of Medicine) and perhaps of the era. As the one thing needful for society, the familiar Swiftian pair—sweetness and light—is replaced by the phrase "the spirit of lucidity."

In developing the potential value of the college to stimulate the life of the spirit in Liverpool, Arnold touched on the weakness of the expanding industrial centers of northern England—"'the hideousness, the immense ennui,' of a type of life too prevalent both here and in America." Joining America with England in a small way softens the indictment by spreading it; for, by making an equation between the countries, Arnold makes any criticism of the one at least obliquely a criticism of the other.

In May, 1882, the month in which he delivered the annual Rede Lecture to a crowded hall at Cambridge University, he also published in the *Nineteenth Century* his essay "A Word about America." He was pleased to think that his "flair" had served him well in writing it and that the younger Henry James had found it so persuasive that he declined the invitation of James Knowles, the editor, to make a reply.[16] In this essay Arnold makes use, tellingly, of his equation: "I have long accustomed myself to regard the people of the United States as just the same people with ourselves, as simply 'the English on the other side of the Atlantic.' "[17]

The inherent satirical stroke, which Arnold himself explains later in the essay, is that he had in *Culture and Anarchy* described American society as like the British—with the Barbarians left out, and the Populace nearly left out: as a nation of Philistines. He chooses Henry James's Philistine Mr. Striker in *Roderick Hudson* to exemplify the typical American. While the lecture defines Arnold's vision of America as Philistia and permits him to spar briefly with Thomas Wentworth Higginson and James Russell Lowell, who had taken umbrage at his superiority of tone towards America, the real aim of the lecture is to deliver the English middle class from its bondage to Protestant sectarianism and to challenge its insufficient provision for secondary education, its limited range of intellect, and its limited sense for beauty.

Although Arnold expressed doubts in "A Word about America" concerning his ability to visit the country, he wrote to James Russell Lowell in August, 1882, that friends had proposed to him that a lecture tour there would raise the amount he needed to pay off a debt. The obligation was incurred by his borrowing money to settle his son Richard's Oxford debts and to pay for a voyage to Australia from which Richard had lately returned.[18] Arrangements proceeded into the spring and summer of 1883. "If I make my lowly grave by the banks of the Connecticut River, you will sometimes remember me?" he wrote wistfully to John Morley.[19] In October he sailed with his wife and his older daughter Lucy on the Cunard liner, the *Servia*. Andrew Carnegie with his secretary met them on their arrival in New York City on October 15 and hurried them off to the Windsor Hotel for the beginning of a long and fatiguing but financially profitable tour. The recently organized Authors Club of New York made him its first honorary member on October 24.

On Tuesday, October 30, he gave his first lecture, "Numbers," in New York City at Chickering Hall. General Ulysses S. Grant was among those in the audience. On November 7, introduced by the aging Oliver Wendell Holmes, he repeated the lecture in Boston. The tour took him to a number of New England colleges —Dartmouth, Wellesley, Amherst; he read his poetry in Sanders

Theatre at Harvard; and he lectured, among other places, in Worcester, New Haven, Brooklyn, Washington, Richmond, Baltimore, Philadelphia, Buffalo, Cleveland, Chicago, Milwaukee, St. Louis, Cincinnati, Toronto, Ottawa, Montreal, and Albany. He was entertained by Vanderbilts and Delanos; by Dr. Holmes; by Charles Eliot Norton; by Emerson's widow, who displayed "manners of high distinction," and by Emerson's daughter; and by Phillips Brooks. He met John Hay; Rufus Choates' charming daughters; "dear old Whittier"; "a pleasant Professor Child, a great authority on ballad poetry"; and P. T. Barnum.

He gathered impressions of America—"the unbounded hospitality and kindness"; everywhere the greater "buoyancy, enjoyment, and freedom from constraint" as compared with the middle class in England; everywhere a love of publicity and being "on the go"; the beauty of Hollywood Cemetery in Richmond—"such magnolias, such redberried hollies, such oaks!"; the legislature in session in the Capitol in Richmond—"the dirt, untidiness, and spitting were quite Southern here, and remind one of all that Trollope and Dickens say"; a breakfast party at Andover with "professors and their wives—coffee, fruit, fish-balls, potatoes, hashed veal, and mince-pies, with rolls and butter."[20] "Quebec," he wrote at the end of the tour, "is the most interesting thing by much that I have seen on this Continent, and I think I would sooner be a poor priest in Quebec than a rich hog-merchant in Chicago."[21] The Authors Club held a farewell reception in his honor on the evening of February 28, at which Arnold gave in his brief address Jamesian advice to pursue the profession of letters seriously. The Arnolds returned to England on the *Servia* in March, 1884.

The impact of this extensive and widely advertised tour was varied. Arnold's adverse opinions about America were well known, as was his sometimes condescending manner. His initial inaudible delivery in New York City was noted. Andrew Carnegie thought his speaking manner was "ministerial." His appearance attracted journalistic attention. The New York *Tribune* reported on October 31 that he was "tall, well formed, with an air of high breeding and refinement, but his face is not sicklied o'er with the pale cast of thought. It is a plain, kindly, face, with old-fashioned, mutton-chop whiskers, keen grey eyes, and a flexible mouth.["]22 Arnold told his daughter Nelly, "A Detroit newspaper compared me, as I stooped now and then to look at my manuscript on a music stool, to 'an elderly bird pecking at grapes on a trellis.' "23

John Henry Raleigh points out in *Matthew Arnold and American Culture* that, among the major American writers of the latter half of the century only Melville and Emerson, who died in 1882, and Henry James, Jr., were enthusiastic admirers of Arnold. The intelligently sympathetic estimate of Arnold by James in the *English Illustrated Magazine* for January, 1884, coincided with the lecture tour. On the other hand, James Russell Lowell, E. C. Stedman, Mark Twain, William Dean Howells, and Walt Whitman expressed widely ranging degrees of reserve. And the officials of Princeton and of Haverford College, disapproving of his heterodoxy, refused to sponsor his lectures.

On his side Arnold had for many years expressed opinions that in themselves and in their tone were nettling, however true. The disparaging references to America in the private letters to Clough about mid-century are qualified by an air of banter, but Arnold delighted in reiterating with a high degree of seriousness Jules Michelet's phrase about the harsh lack of intelligence of the Americans—"la dure inintelligence des Anglo-Americains."24 "They me font l'effet of a nation not having on a wedding-garment," Arnold told Clough.25 Publicly in *The Popular Education of France* (1861), while he confessed to more than respect, to "warm interest" in "a great nation of English blood," he deplored American self-conceit; and he said, "This is the capital misfortune of the American people, that it is a people which has had to grow up without ideals."26 Later in *A French Eton* (1863) while he approved the readiness of Americans to accept centralized state action in education, he had with uncustomary hardness rejoiced, as we have noted, in the refining of the American spirit "in the furnace of civil war." His cautionary essay "A World about America" was not wholly flattering to "that Paradise of the Sects," nor to Colonel Thomas Wentworth Higginson, a very considerable patriot of American letters. After Arnold's return to England, the indignant Higginson described as "humiliating," what he believed, though not entirely accurately, to be "the reverential attention visible in the American press when Matthew Arnold was kind enough to stand on tip-toe upon our lecture-platform and apply his measuring-tape to the great shade of Emerson."[27]

The formal message that Arnold brought to the United States was delivered in three lectures, collected under the title *Discourses in America* (1885): "Numbers; or, the Majority and the Remnant," "Literature and Science," and "Emerson." Posterity has not concurred in Arnold's judgment when he told G. W. Russell in 1887 "that *Discourses in America* was the book by which, of all his prose-writings, he should most wish to be remembered." Yet the judgment may serve to sharpen the reader's alertness to what Arnold regarded as his themes of greatest validity.

In "Numbers," Arnold's role is entirely that of moralist. He described it himself as "a sort of lay sermon." Beginning with Dr. Johnson's barbed maxim "Patriotism is the last refuge of a scoundrel" and with Bishop Butler's fatalistic saying, "Things are what they are and the consequences of them will be what they will be; why, then, should we desire to be deceived?," Arnold appeals to his American audience to recognize the sobering validity of Isaiah's prophecy: "Though thy people Israel be as the sand of the sea, only a remnant of them shall return."[28] Through an arithmetical process, whose strangeness Lionel Trilling has noted, Arnold reached the optimistic conclusion that the large population of America would produce a group of men and women whose spiritual enlightenment would suffice to preserve the culture of the whole. In Israel and Athens, the saving remnant had not been sufficient; but the hope is that in modern society the remnant may increase in power, a hope allied to Arnold's sense of an intellectually ameliorating middle class.

The state is saved ultimately by its devotion to moral good. The failure to be just and to be "amiable" is England's current failure in Ireland. The recent failure of France—evidenced by its popular novels, its theater, its press—is its failure to hold a sufficiently rigorous sexual morality. Even Renan had lately proclaimed, "Nature cares nothing for chastity."[29] Lubricity—the term Arnold floats in this essay—has become the French Diana of Ephesus. The United States too has its characteristic dangers "in the absence of the discipline of respect; in hardness and materialism, exaggeration and boastfulness; in a false smartness, a false audacity, a want of soul and delicacy."[30] Is there hope for America in addition to its numbers? Yes, for there are, Arnold proposes quite startlingly, its discipline of Puritanism and its Germanic stock—a stock, "as my father said more than fifty years ago, . . . 'of the most moral races of men that the world has yet seen, with the soundest laws, the least violent passions, the fairest domestic and civil virtues.' "[31]

The defect of "Numbers" is partly one of tone, but this essay also exposes Arnold's frequent neglect to sharpen his definitions, and consequently his concepts. Arnold is effective in expressing attitudes, but he is very weak in examining causal relations. The rhetorical play that he makes with the idea of a new goddess of Lubricity has an urbanity that is lacking in Tennyson's contemporary tirade against French culture in "Locksley Hall Sixty Years After" (1886); nevertheless the recurrent air of condescension by the speaker towards his alien audience spoils the effectiveness of his message.

In December Arnold wrote to an English friend: "Here in New England every one is full of the Education question, and of the contest between letters and science more particularly; and all the country places want to hear me on Literature and Science. When I get to the great towns I have to give the lecture on Numbers."[32] "Literature and Science," a revised form of the Rede Lecture of 1882 that Arnold had delivered at Cambridge University, was given for the last time to a large and attentive audience at Dundee in October, 1884.

The debate between the "two cultures" was far from new even in the nineteenth century when Thomas Henry Huxley delivered his lecture on science and culture at Birmingham on October 1, 1880. Perhaps no intellectual debate was more of the century; originally, it was the intellectual counterpart of the Industrial Revolution. The opposition between poetry and science set up by Thomas Love Peacock's *Four Ages of Poetry* and Shelley's *Defense of Poetry* was part of the debate; and in 1837, the year of Victoria's coronation, Macaulay made his dramatic distinction between the ancient Classical school and the Utilitarian School of Fruit and Progress; in 1848 De Quincey made his distinction between the Literature of Knowledge and the Literature of Power. But, in its more classic form for us, the debate is post-Darwinian. Huxley gaily challenged Arnold directly with phrases about "Levites in charge of the ark of culture" and "epistles to the Philistines." Arnold's Rede Lecture was his ingratiating reply.

Plato's advice in the ninth book of the *Republic* establishes the essential point of the lecture: "An intelligent man will prize those studies which result in his soul getting soberness, righteousness, and wisdom, and will less value the others." With a dégagé manner Arnold leads the argument back to his early essay "The Function of Criticism at the Present Time" as he reminds his audience of his "observation to the effect that in our culture, the aim being *to know ourselves and the world*, we have, as the means to this end, *to know the best which has been thought and said in the world.*"[33]

A study of literature best serves this humanistic end, but literature is conceived not as *belles lettres* but as a way of knowing the "life and genius" of a people and their values. Beyond this Arnold argues that the experience of literature appeals to a psychological need of human nature—to what he calls the "the instinct of self-preservation in humanity";[34] this is the meaning of what Diotima taught Socrates; this is the impulse satisfied by what appeals to our sense for conduct and our sense for beauty. This is what Spinoza meant when he said, "Man's happiness consists in his being able to preserve his own essence."[35]

This need is not satisfied when men have assimilated "the proposition that their ancestor was 'a hairy quadruped furnished with a tail and pointed ears, probably arboreal in his habits.' "[36] The stream of tendency is on the side of the humanities: "The 'hairy quadruped furnished with a tail and pointed ears, probably arboreal in his habits,' this good fellow carried hidden in his nature, apparently, something destined to develop into a necessity for humane letters. Nay, more; we seem finally to be even led to the further conclusion that our hairy ancestor carried in his nature, also, a necessity for Greek."[37]

The lecture "Emerson" offended American audiences because of the carefully circumscribed limit of Arnold's praise. Emerson is denied greatness as a poet, as an essayist, as a systematic thinker. He is praised in association with Marcus Aurelius as a moralist who was capable by his reflections of molding the spirit. In its way, the lecture is an example of Arnold's determination to achieve objectivity in criticism, to avoid dangers of personal and historical estimates that he had defined in his essay "The Study of Poetry" (1880). To be a molder of the spirit is, of course, for Arnold in itself high praise. His strategy to mollify the patriotic critic who demanded greater praise is not to make concessions but to make disarming and flattering associations with Emerson's name—Carlyle, Goethe, Senancour, Marcus Aurelius; and, while he himself confesses to the strong enchantment of personal feelings as an Oxford undergraduate toward John Henry Newman, to allow that Emerson makes a like claim upon Americans.

Upon his return to England Arnold promised for the November or December issue of the *Nineteenth Century* a new essay "A Word More about America." He proposed printing it with "A Word about America" and with the three other lectures as a book *American Addresses.* "A Word about America" appeared in the *Nineteenth Century* in February, 1885. The book, containing only the lectures, was published as *Discourses in America* in June. But Arnold had not yet done with the United States or with lectures about America. During the lecture tour his daughter Lucy met and subsequently married Frederick W. Whitridge of New York City; and Arnold returned with his wife for a second visit to see his daughter and granddaughter in the spring and summer of 1886. He lectured at the University of Pennsylvania in June, but the summer he spent chiefly at Stockbridge, Massachusetts, following with interest the difficult progress of Anglo-Irish affairs, and pursuing with enthusiasm his devotion to wild flowers. From Stockbridge he wrote to his sister Fan, a fellow enthusiast: "We were perpetually stopping the carriage in the woods through which we drove, the flowers were so attractive; we settled that you would be particularly struck with the *Gerardia* flower and the *Desmodium.* But I think myself you would be so plunged in the varieties of the golden rod and the aster, that you would go mad over them and be left in an asylum."[38]

Arnold, after his return to England in September, 1886, had one final word to say about America—a lecture he delivered on January 31, 1888, at Hull and published as "Civilisation in the United States" in the *Nineteenth Century* for April of the same year. The small Boston publishing firm, Cupples and Hurd, gathered this essay, a desultory two-part review of General Grant's *Personal Memoirs,* "A Word about America," and "A Word More about America" into the book called *Civilization in the United States: First and Last Impressions of America* (1888).

"A Word More about America" proposes to record some "new and modifying impressions" about the United States. Arnold grants that he was more highly impressed than he had anticipated by the interrelations of federal, state and municipal governments; that he found the Philistines more lively than their English counterparts, taking their rich men less seriously than the European. But the essay is much less a corrective of earlier impressions than an instrument for opening attacks on indecisive British foreign policy, on an inactive session of the House of Commons, and on an embittering Irish policy. "A Word More about America" is of negligible interest for Arnold's views on America, or indeed on the now remote political problems of 1884; but it shows with what concern he was following the political matters that he wrote about in the next few years.

In "Civilization in the United States" Arnold returned to the "human problem"—as distinct from the social and political. He returned in effect to the grounds of the moralist—a concern with the humanization of man in society. With no loss of his old urbanity, he analyzes the propensity to boasting, the avidness for news, the brashness of its journalism, the lack of "interest" in the American cultural scene, the need for self-criticism, the insensitiveness reflected in the place-names—Briggsvilles, Higginsvilles, Jacksonvilles. And we are back in the Arnoldian world of 1865—"by the Ilissus there was no Wragg, poor thing!" The final appeal, however, is not to the United States only; it is the affirmation of Arnold's existential commitment: "Except a man be born *from above,* he cannot have part in the society of the future."

CHAPTER 9

"A Far-Set Goal"

I *Late Political Essays*

ON NOVEMBER 12, 1886, Matthew Arnold retired after thirty-five years as an inspector of schools. The teachers of the Westminster District commemorated the occasion with the presentation of a silver claret jug and a salver. "I was afraid of a tea-service," he confided to his daughter in the United States. "I could get through life with a wooden spoon and platter. . . ."[1] Modifying this ascetic image of himself, however, he added that, when he was asked what he would really like, if he didn't care for plate, he had answered, "A carriage, a pair of horses, and to have them kept for me!"

Retirement from school inspecting was not withdrawal from his engagement to promote radically, in his way, the general good. Lionel Trilling has proposed that Arnold's career was "spent in evaluating the French Revolution"; in his late years he was most energetically the champion of its social principles of equality and fraternity in their spiritual modes. He expressed clearly his deep sense of social obligation in a letter to his youngest sister, who, we surmise, had cast herself in the role of Lady Bountiful:

I heard with great interest of your Christmas, and perhaps there is nothing in which one may more safely employ oneself, or which brings one, and properly brings, so much happiness as beneficence. But do you not feel sometimes anxious to attack the condition of things which seems to bring about the evils on which your beneficence has to be exercised? When once you have got it into your head that this condition *does* in great measure bring the evils about, and that it is in great measure remediable, I think one can hardly rest satisfied with merely alleviating the evils that arise under it.[2]

Arnold's best poetry originates in his intuitive sense of man's individualism and his metaphysical isolation; his most characteristic prose, as a literary and religious and social critic, originates in his sense of the need to unite men in a society founded on rationalism and humanistic values. In effect he always wished to be able to ask himself "without shame," as he said shortly before his first visit to America, "Joseph de Maistre's beautiful question, 'En quoi ai-j'avancé l'oeuvre générale, et que reste-t-il de moi en bien ou en mal?' "[3] ("In what way have I advanced the general work that is to be done, and what shall remain of me for good or for evil?")

The problems of Ireland provided an area of the general good to which Arnold turned during the last years of his life. Detached from party, he viewed himself as a disinterested observer of "the state and prospects of our civilisation." His interest in Ireland extended at least as far back as the Oxford lectures on Celtic literature in 1866. He expressed sympathies that were more politically focused in *Culture and Anarchy* (1869), where the chapter called "Our Liberal Practitioners" supported, for the sake of reason and justice, the reapportioning of church property in Ireland among the leading denominations. In *Mixed Essays* (1879) and in *Irish Essays and Others* (1882) Arnold also included several articles that he had published in the *Fortnightly Review* or the *Nineteenth Century*.

Admittedly sympathetic with the great historical religions, he wrote in behalf of a state-supported Roman Catholic university for Ireland; he argued for the systematic expropriation by a State Commission of the property of "bad landlords"; and he urged a state system for middle-class education, for, though the Irish middle class might have "quicker" minds than the English middle class with its fear of state intervention, the Irish had "a defective type of religion, a narrow range of intellect and knowledge, a stunted sense of beauty, a low standard of manners."[4] Ultimately the aims of educator, statesman, poet, critic met for Arnold in a single Socratic goal—"that the whole body of society should come to live with a life worthy to be called *human*."[5]

Awareness of this goal gives constancy to the ambivalent expressions we can find in Arnold regarding the long future of

Western culture. Within one context he could affirm, "Instinctively, however slowly, the human spirit struggles toward the light; and the adoptions and rejections of its agents by the multitude are never wholly blind and capricious, but have a meaning."[6] In another context he could admit, "In the immense procession of ages, what countless communities have arisen and sunk unknown, and even the most famous nation, perhaps, is only for its day."[7] But in the interim, whatever the alternatives, there remained for man one clear obligation: to promote sanity in human affairs.

In May, 1886, the month in which Arnold sailed on the *Umbria* for his second visit to the United States, his article "The Nadir of Liberalism" appeared in the *Nineteenth Century*. Although he had thought of this as "a last political article," it was the first of six, including two letters to the London *Times*, that he wrote as he anxiously watched the progress of Gladstone's Home Rule policy for Ireland. It was followed in the *Nineteenth Century* in 1887 by "The Zenith of Conservatism" in the January issue, by "Up to Easter" in May, and by "From Easter to August" in September.

Arnold was a strong opponent of Gladstone's policy. He believed that the proposal for a separate parliament and a separate executive for Ireland would lead to a separate Ireland and that the inequities arising from the land problem, from intolerance toward Roman Catholicism, and from the ill effects of poor education could only be solved by remedial measures grounded in what are essentially the Swiftian ethical virtues of justice, reasonableness, sympathy, open-mindedness, honesty. Arnold believed with Edmund Burke, some of whose writings on Irish affairs he had collected in 1881 as relevant to contemporary issues, that "Irish misery and discontent have been due more to English misgovernment than to Irish faults," and he believed that Home Rule meant increased alienation and that increased alienation meant increased misery.[8]

John Morley once said of Arnold that "his insight into the roots of the Irish case, and the strong persistence with which he pressed the case upon unwilling ears, were in some ways the most remarkable instance of his many-sided and penetrating vision."[9] But Arnold's latest reflections on Irish affairs are rightly described by Lionel Trilling as laborious. While they attest to Arnold's political awareness, they are not politically constructive, and they do not transcend their occasion. Controlled rage informs Swift's indignation against injustice; Arnold's reiterated appeals to quiet, reasonable people achieve only a pale amenity.

II *Essays in Criticism. Second Series*

Arnold's father had died of angina pectoris. Arnold, too, suffered from the disease, to which he alludes in a letter in the spring of 1885—"At present I feel very unlike lawn-tennis, as going fast or going up hill gives me the sense of having a mountain on my chest."[10] In the summer he played tennis again ("I was a little tired but the cool champagne at dinner brought me quite round"[11]), and all one October morning he was proudly gathering baskets of pears and walnuts of his own growing, the mongrel dachshund Kai watching while Max, his "brother dog," tried vainly to get into the cucumber frame where the yellow cat had betaken himself for warmth. Occasional recurrence of warning pains continued through the second American visit—once deterring him from journeying to Bar Harbor from Charles Eliot Norton's summer home at Stockbridge.

Nevertheless, the amiable life reflected in Arnold's family letters and the productiveness of his writing continued—a review for a friend of Johann Tauler's *The Following of Christ*; a review of General Grant's memoirs; essays on Amiel, Tolstoi, Shelley, and Milton for *Macmillan's Magazine*, the *Fortnightly Review*, the *Nineteenth Century*, and the *Century Magazine*; a political article "Disestablishment in Wales" for the *National Review* (March, 1888); and a major article on Charles Sainte-Beuve for the ninth edition of the *Encyclopedia Britannica*, that still, anonymous and abridged, adorns the 1960 printing of that work.

In mid-January, 1888, George L. Craik, of Macmillan and Company, proposed to Arnold that he assemble a new volume of collected papers. He responded at once with the idea of "a purely literary volume to go with 'Essays in Criticism' and to be called 'Essays in Criticism Second Series,'"[12] and he drew up a table of contents. On April 14 Arnold went to Liverpool to meet his daughter Lucy Whitridge, who was returning with her daughter

("We have a flock of sheep—Southdowns, with fine black-faced lambs—in the paddock; what a sight for the Midget!" Arnold wrote his sister[13]). On the afternoon of Sunday, April 15, he leaped over a low fence in happy anticipation of meeting his family, and fell dead. He was buried with his three sons at Laleham. Dick, his surviving son, and Mrs. Arnold saw the projected volume through the press. His friend John Duke Coleridge, now Lord Chief Justice, contributed a brief prefatory note.

Essays in Criticism, Second Series was published in November, 1888. It contains nine essays: the general introduction and the introductions to Gray and Keats from T. H. Ward's anthology *The English Poets* (1880); the prefaces to Arnold's selections from Wordsworth (1879) and from Byron (1881); a speech on Milton which Arnold had recently given in 1888 at the unveiling of a memorial window in St. Margaret's Church, Westminster; a review of Tolstoi's *Anna Karenina* (1887); his reflections on Amiel's *Journal* (1887) that his niece Mrs. Humphry Ward had translated; and an essay on Shelley (1888), precipitated by his adverse reaction to Edward Dowden's *Life of Shelley*. Arnold had intended to write a second article on Shelley, and in January, 1888, he had "one or two other literary articles" in mind.

Less assertive than Arnold's first critical essay—the Preface to the poems of 1853—less polemical in origin than the *Essays in Criticism* of 1865, and less amusingly jaunty in tone than some of them, these nine essays, nevertheless, complete his career with remarkable symmetry. They express a critical position that he had formulated in early remarks on the choice of appropriate and interesting human actions, on the grand style, on disinterestedness, on "the best that is thought and known in the world," and on literature as a criticism of life. They have their own unity as serving the cause of civilizing men; making more discriminating their sensibilities; and aiding, as Arnold defines his aim in his so frequently repeated phrase, in "the humanisation of man in society." They continue, as part of the endeavor to civilize, the exposure of Philistine insensibility.

For example, in the essay on Tolstoi a parallel between Russia and the United States makes possible an ironic attack on American Philistinism as represented by the intellectual complacency of Thomas Wentworth Higginson. In the important essay on Byron, a circuitous discussion of his power as a poet terminates in discussion of his personality; for, as in the 1865 essay on Heine, Arnold turned away from his poetry to interpret him as "a soldier in the war of liberation of humanity," he now turns from Byron's poetry to celebrate him as a "passionate and dauntless soldier" against the sterile domination of the old order. Arnold, who at times anticipated a new spirit in the middle class, could still, in the context of his own reawakened emotions about Byron, cry that "His own aristocratic class, whose cynical make-believe drove him to fury; the great middle class, on whose impregnable Philistinism he shattered himself to pieces, —how little have either of these felt Byron's vital influence!"[14]

"The Study of Poetry," the leading essay in the book, is, with the 1853 Preface and "The Function of Criticism at the Present Time," one of Arnold's three most important critical essays. Frederic Harrison, Arnold's Positivist critic, pronounced that it "should be preserved in our literature as the *norma* or *canon* of right opinion about poetry."[15] Even T. S. Eliot, Arnold's unwilling heir, who was born in the year of his death, conceded in *The Use of Poetry and the Use of Criticism,* that it is—for its economy and authority—a classic of English criticism.[16] Allen Tate in *On the Limits of Poetry* has said that "debased Arnold is the main stream of popular appreciation of poetry."[17]

"The Study of Poetry" was first published in 1880 as the general introduction to T. H. Ward's *The English Poets.* Implicit in its remarkable opening paragraph is Arnold's sense of the dynamics of change in his age, and of the pragmatic character of poetry:

"The future of poetry is immense, because in poetry, where it is worthy of its high destinies, our race, as time goes on, will find an ever surer and surer stay. There is not a creed which is not shaken, not an accredited dogma which is not shown to be questionable, not a received tradition which does not threaten to dissolve. Our religion has materialised itself in the fact, in the supposed fact; it has attached its emotion to the fact, and now the fact is failing it. But for poetry the idea is everything; the rest is a world of illusion, of divine illusion. Poetry attaches its emotion to the idea; the idea *is* the fact. The strongest part of our religion to-day is its unconscious poetry."[18]

This paragraph, like the entire essay, raises issues that, for their resolution, look in many directions. Terms like "worthy," "high," "destiny," and "divine illusion" have a Pateresque quality, reminding us of Walter Pater's more varied but similar vocabulary of critical terms: "high," "fair," "comely," "grace," "charm," "nobility." And their use invests the critic, whether Arnold or Pater, with a hieratic manner, a mantic role, that in one way bespeaks a direct relationship between art and morality, or in another implies a theory of "art for art's sake." This last direction is supported by Arnold's appeal to "tact," to sensitivity, to "an accent," to "high beauty, worth, and power," when he develops his criterion of "touchstones" in this essay.

But the idea of "art for art's sake" has surprising witnesses; we can, after all, extract from Ruskin's Crown of Wild Olives (1864) the very Wildean pronouncement: "Taste is not only a part and an index of morality, it is the ONLY morality." Moreover, in T. S. Eliot we find an ambivalence similar to that in Arnold between sensibility as an evidence of esthetic education and sensibility as an evidence of a total personality. For example, in Eliot's influential essay on Dante, however much more subtle is the analysis, the appeals to the reader's esthetic response are accompanied by passages that gain power from the ethical attitudes that they imply; and, when Eliot criticizes Tennyson's phrase about the sea which "moans round with many voices" as "too poetical in comparison with Dante, to be the highest poetry," he is using an Arnoldian critical adjective with Arnoldian ambiguity of meaning.[19]

In "The Study of Poetry" the sense of fragmentation in the age, of the loss of certainty, which Arnold expressed as a crisis of religious faith in "Dover Beach," is extended to a wider application: ". . . our religion, parading evidences such as those on which the popular mind relies now; our philosophy, pluming itself on its reasonings about causation and finite and infinite being; what are these but the shadows and dreams and false shows of knowledge."[20] Like Pater, Arnold at moments is divided between the claims of the absolute and those of a dissolvent relativity, between Sophoclean affirmation of a universe in which the God does not grow old and Euripidean skepticism: "For it costs little to believe that the divine, whatever it is, has power, and that what has been accepted over a long time is eternal, and rooted in the nature of things."

Yet the preponderance of Arnold's thought weighs in favor of a stabilizing ethical morality that will increasingly enlighten more men in more numerous areas of their sensitivity. The injunction of "The Function of Criticism"—to see things as in themselves they really are—is given a more strictly literary application in "The Study of Poetry." To Ruskin's "pathetic" fallacy, Arnold adds his terms; he shrewdly cautions against the historic fallacy and the personal fallacy—chauvinistic and subjective causes of aberrations in literary estimates.

Latent in this essay are two prescriptions for avoiding these errors. He speaks in a famous phrase of poetry "as a criticism of life under the conditions fixed for such a criticism by the laws of poetic truth and poetic beauty."[21] The critical direction from "the laws of poetic truth and poetic beauty" leads back to Coleridge, and forward to T. E. Hulme and the New Criticism. In Arnold it remains an isolated aperçu, like his proposition that poetry "is thought and art in one." However, without a vocabulary to analyze the internal operations of poetry, or the power to devise one, Arnold followed his bent as moralist to emphasize the idea—sometimes extractable; sometimes, as with the "touchstones," intrinsic with the style—where the organic relation of idea and expression is felt but not articulated.

Arnold assumes a class of poetry that can be defined as "truly excellent." To aid us as readers in the skill of recognition, he proposes to lodge in our minds certain passages or lines as "infallible" touchstones. For example, there are Hamlet's words to Horatio—

> If thou didst ever hold me in thy heart,
> Absent thee from felicity awhile,
> And in this harsh world draw thy breath in pain
> To tell my story . . . ;

or Milton's

> And courage never to submit or yield
> And what is else not to be overcome. . . ;

or, in *The Divine Comedy,* Piccarda's

In la sua voluntade è nostra pace;
(In His will is our peace)

or Ugolino's

Io no piangera; sì dentro impietrai
Piangevan elli.

It is not to be supposed that Arnold did not know that the force of Ugolino's words is not conveyed by the translation he gives: "I wailed not, so of stone I grew within;—*they* wailed." But for want of stylistic analysis, we are left perceiving that these and his other *loci* present ethical situations; for them to be meaningful, we must be able to provide or imagine a context in which some Promethean defiance, or Stoic endurance, or deeply inward acquiescence displays a victorious response to enveloping daemonic forces or to the blindness of circumstance.

The recommendation about the "touchstones" is followed by Arnold's brisk survey of English poetry, fortified in its moralistic emphasis by an interpretation of Aristotle's dictum that poetry has a higher truth and a higher seriousness than history—but what is "high," what are "truth" and "seriousness" we ask in vain. Chaucer fails to achieve the "accent" of Piccarda's acquiescent line; Shakespeare and Milton are bypassed as being established classics by a "universal" estimate; Dryden and Pope are examined and dismissed in a passage which Arnold never surpassed for bias or for stylistic brilliance: "We are to regard Dryden as the puissant and glorious founder, Pope as the splendid high priest, of our age of prose and reason, of our excellent and indispensable eighteenth century."[22] Remarkably, Arnold's critical mode itself becomes magisterial, his style wittily balanced and antithetical as he deals with Dryden and Pope—and Gray, both here and in the larger essay about him. Burns, too, fails to rise to the height of Piccarda's renunciation in *The Divine Comedy.* Worse than Burns, Shelley fails by his ethereality. Byron and Wordsworth are reserved for consideration elsewhere.

The essay concludes with its resonant formula insuring the

permanent value of literature—"the instinct of self-preservation in humanity." The best praise of this essay comes from F. R. Leavis, who in "Matthew Arnold" in *The Importance of Scrutiny* records his own experience: "And with whatever reservations, protests, and irritations we read 'The Study of Poetry,' it is impossible in reading it (I find) not to recognize that we have to do with an extraordinarily distinguished mind in complete possession of its purpose and pursuing it with easy mastery— that, in fact, we are reading a great critic."[23]

Because of the broad survey of literary history it includes and because of its formulation of standards of judgment, "The Study of Poetry" is the most important single essay in this last book of criticism. Yet inevitably the attention that Arnold gives to major English poets, especially those of the Romantic period, also made the volume widely popular; and the frequent anthologizing of the essays on Keats, Wordsworth, Byron, and Shelley has made it widely familiar and influential.

These essays exemplify the Arnoldian principles of criticism in action: the insistence that literary work exhibit its author's integrated moral and esthetic sensibility, and the application of "tact" and taste to discern through style this moral wholeness. In the long run, Arnold, like Longinus, wants the literary performance to manifest the ring of a great soul—and the great soul is recognizable by manifesting its grasp of unchanging moral verities. Arnold would agree with Dr. Samuel Johnson's celebrated dictum in his "Preface to Shakespeare": "The pleasures of sudden wonder are soon exhausted, and the mind can only repose on the stability of truth."[24]

In these essays Arnold catches something of the authoritativeness of statement that is a part of the compelling force of Johnsonian judicial criticism. Arnold—after deploring in the essay on Keats the publication of the passionate letters to Fanny Brawne and Keats's sensuousness as a poet in contrast to Shakespeare's wholeness—concludes, quoting Keats's famous words, " 'I think,' he said humbly, 'I shall be among the English poets after my death.' He is; he is with Shakespeare."[25] In the essay on Wordsworth, in which Arnold rejects the hedonism of the recently popular *Rubáiyát of Omar Khayyám*, he pronounces: "A poetry of revolt against moral ideas is a poetry of revolt against *life*; a poetry of indifference to moral ideas is a poetry of indifference to *life*."[26]

In the essay on Byron, Arnold praises Wordsworth and Byron as the two major poets of his century—Wordsworth, as a source of joy and consolation for mankind, Byron, for his sincerity and strength. And he concludes: "Keats had probably, indeed, a more consummate poetic gift than either of them; but he died having produced too little and being as yet too immature to rival them. I for my part can never even think of equalling with them any other of their contemporaries;—either Coleridge, poet and philosopher wrecked in a mist of opium; or Shelley, beautiful and ineffectual angel, beating in the void his luminous wings in vain."[27]

Pronouncements like these induce us to suspend, at least momentarily, our critical judgment. Sometimes, as in the instance of Keats, we may continue to assent; sometimes, as regards Coleridge, we may demand to know more fully what Arnold means; sometimes, as in the case of Shelley, perverse though the judgments now seem, we must recognize that they had the power to become for a generation or so a part of our literary mythology.

Although *Essays in Criticism, Second Series* appeals for literary judgment to matters of style and taste and ethical content, it also includes another continuing concern of Arnold: his campaign against Philistinism. This is a major theme in the essay on Byron. Arnold's Byron, like his Heine, is a hero in the war for the liberation of man from the tyrannies of society and of his own nature; therefore, the sympathy of Arnold for Byron is profound. The young Arnold felt the anguish of Byronic rebelliousness although his intellect rejected it as ineffectual. The Arnold of the 1880's admired the integrity and the persistency of Byron's satirical attack against the closed mind. An outward buoyancy of hope characterizes Arnold's usual later attitude towards the English middle class. The essay on Byron, however, betrays a passionate despair that makes this peroration as relevant to himself as it is to Byron:

As the inevitable break-up of the old order comes, as the English middle-class slowly awakens from its intellectual sleep of two centuries, as our actual present world, to which this sleep has condemned us, shows itself more clearly,—our world of an aristocracy materialised and null, a middle-class purblind and hideous, a lower class crude and brutal,—we shall turn our eyes again, and to more purpose, upon this passionate and dauntless soldier of a forlorn hope, who, ignorant of the future and unconsoled by its promises, nevertheless waged against the conservation of the old impossible world so fiery battle; waged it till he fell,—waged it with such splendid and imperishable excellence of sincerity and strength.[28]

Reading the *Essays in Criitcism, Second Series* today, we are surprised to find so little critical analysis in what is officially literary criticism. We inevitably share the ambivalent responses of many contemporary critics to Arnold—T. S. Eliot, I. A. Richards, F. R. Leavis, Allen Tate, W. K. Wimsatt, and Cleanth Brooks. The critical road leading from Arnold in the direction of the early generation of American humanists represented by Irving Babbitt and Paul Elmer More has proven so unrewarding, but the direction toward the kind of analysis that Arnold never undertook has been so productive of insights that we regret Arnold's inability to follow it. His often circular arguments, his "touchstones," his special pleading are severe limitations. This response would be damaging if Arnold were rightly to be seen as having been in his essays primarily a literary critic, as having represented himself primarily as one. In fact he was much more continuously a critic of the moral sensibility of man in society. Like the Heine and the Byron whom he celebrated and admired, Arnold waged a perpetual campaign against the provincialisms of his age. Like most satirists, he was a moralist; like all moralists, he was profoundly in earnest. We come again to H. V. Routh's interesting suggestion that Arnold was a moralist who has been mistaken for a literary critic.

III *Conclusion*

Matthew Arnold survives not only for the ideas he expressed, but also for his mode of expressing them. He survives, moreover, as the engaging personality that he was for his friends. Referring to Arnold's second American tour, Henry James, Jr., wrote from Milan on December 6, 1886, to Charles Eliot Norton: "I saw

Matt Arnold the other night, and he spoke very genially of you and of his visit to Ashfield—very *affectionately*, too, of George Curtis—which I loudly echoed. M. A. said of Stockbridge and the summer life thereabouts, etc. (with his chin in the air)— 'Yes, yes—it's a proof that it's attaching that one thinks of it again—one thinks of it again.' This was amiably sublime and amiably characteristic."[29] The charm of his character expresses itself through the friendliness of the letters and through the several voices of the poems and the essays—calm, inquiring, compassionate, ironic, rational, urbane, satirical, never outraged, but occasionally outrageous in self-assurance.

E. B. Burgum, whose fine essay "The Humanism of Matthew Arnold" has seemingly been forgotten in the reaction against Marxist critics of the 1930's, defined very well the characteristic pose of Arnold as satirist. Arnold assumes, Burgum said, that his reader is "an aristocrat like himself." "That he may reduce the appearance of egotism in himself and arouse it in his readers, Arnold shrewdly defines them as a little group, at the center of which he discovers himself standing disinterestedly, turning a disapproving eye upon the mob of barbarians, philistines, and populace in the midst of which they perform the miracle of surviving."[30] This stance, which irritated many contemporary readers, also irritates some readers today. But it is not Arnold's only stance, nor was it taken in the interests of egotism. Like the yellow gloves and dandified airs of the Oxford undergraduate, it concealed a private Arnold—one revealed to readers of his religious writings and his *Note-Books*, with their meditational texts from the Bible, Bishop Wilson, Thomas à Kempis, Goethe, among others. Arnold's view of civilization was in a large measure the inculcation of an acceptable ethical morality; he shared the interest of Wordsworth, in the Preface to *Lyrical Ballads*, in enlarging the capabilities of human beings for sensitive and intelligent conduct. The *Note-Books* confirm what Arnold once said about a reader who misconstrued him: "If A. F. had read my books he would know that I have always insisted that the only right way to an outward transformation was through an inward one, and that the business for us and for our age was the latter."[31]

In the preface to the second edition of his important study of

Arnold, Lionel Trilling very eloquently expressed his consciousness of Arnold's relevance for us: that is, that he stood "for the intellectual virtues that are required by a complex society if it is to survive. . . ."[32] Yet while Arnold reaches the modern age in many ways, he is also very much a Victorian. This is not only apparent in the topical nature of his facetious allusions to subjects like the Burial Bill or the question of marriage with a deceased wife's sister, or of his serious references, as to the decay of faith. He is Victorian in his earnestness; in his esteem for the "plain virtues" of strength and honesty; in his personal reticence; in his admiration for "backbone, serious energy, and power of honest work"—in which he thought the Italians were lacking; in the great pleasure he took in Gladstone's praise that he was "doing very great good"; in his concern for progress; in his interest in historic process; and in his declaration—despite his great cosmopolitanism—"I should be sorry to be a Frenchman, German, or American, or anything but an Englishman; but I know that this native instinct which other nations, too, have does not prove one's superiority, but that one has to achieve this by undeniable excellent performance."[33]

Essentially, Arnold transcends his time by virtue of the integrity of his poetic statement and the sanity of his evaluative judgment. He discerned a modern Wasteland and the existential dilemma of the individual. He discerned a way out through commitment to the intellectual enlightenment of society. He engages us as a coherent figure whose wide-ranging interests are controlled by the conviction that reason and patient individual endeavor will always create civilization out of conditions of turbulence and of change.

Notes and References

Chapter One

1. Henry James, Jr., "Matthew Arnold," *English Illustrated Magazine*, I (January, 1884), 241.
2. *Ibid.*, pp. 241-42.
3. *Letters of Matthew Arnold, 1848-1888*, ed. G. W. E. Russell (2 vols. London, 1895), II, 143. (Hereafter referred to as *Letters*.)
4. "Mr. Arnold's New Poems," *Fortnightly Review*, VIII (October, 1867), 425.
5. *Letters*, II, 4.
6. *Letters*, I, 2-3.
7. Arthur P. Stanley, *The Life and Correspondence of Thomas Arnold, D.D.* (2 vols. London, 1844), I, 92-93.
8. E. L. Woodward, *The Age of Reform, 1815-1870* (Oxford, 1938), p. 466.
9. Stanley, I, 55. Dr. Arnold was awarded the degree of B.D. in March 1828 and that of D.D. in December 1828.
10. John Taylor Coleridge, *A Memoir of the Rev. John Keble* (2 vols. Oxford and London, 1869), I, 133.
11. *Ibid.*, I, 183.
12. Stanley, I, 116
13. *Ibid.*, I, 94.
14. *Ibid.*
15. Thomas Arnold, *Passages in a Wandering Life* (London, 1900), p. vi.
16. Stanley, I, 285.
17. *Annual Register*, 1842 (London), p. 72.
18. Stanley, I, 290.
19. *Ibid.*, II, 388.
20. *The Letters of Matthew Arnold to Arthur Hugh Clough*, ed. H. F. Lowry (London and New York, 1932), p. 145, note 3. (Hereafter referred to as *Letters to Clough*.) Lionel Trilling, *Matthew Arnold*, (New York, 1939), p. 18, records that Dr. Arnold once took Matthew to meet Southey at Greta Bank. Southey shook hands and said, "So now you've seen a live poet!"

21. E. K. Chambers, *Matthew Arnold. A Study.* (Oxford, 1947), p. 5.

22. H. F. Lowry, *Matthew Arnold and the Modern Spirit* (Princeton, N. J., 1941), p. 5.

23. Kenneth Allott, "A Birthday Exercise by Matthew Arnold," *Notes and Queries*, n.s. V (May, 1958), 225.

24. Arnold Whitridge, *Dr. Arnold of Rugby* (New York, 1928), p. 41.

25. Iris E. Sells, *Matthew Arnold and France: the Poet* (Cambridge, England, 1935), pp. 257-58.

26. C. B. Tinker and H. F. Lowry, *The Poetry of Matthew Arnold: A Commentary* (London and New York, 1940), pp. 322-23. (Hereafter referred to as *Commentary*.)

27. See *Letters to Clough*, p. 24.

28. F. M. Müller, *Auld Lang Syne* (New York, 1898), pp. 128-29.

29. Quoted in Alan Harris, "Matthew Arnold: The Unknown Years," *Nineteenth Century and After*, CXIII (April, 1933), 501.

30. E. H. Coleridge, *Life and Correspondence of John Duke Lord Coleridge* (2 vols. London, 1904), I, 124.

31. *Ibid.*, I, 129.

32. *Ibid.*, I, 132.

33. *Ibid.*, I, 145-46.

34. Katherine Lake, *Memorials of William Charles Lake* (London, 1901), p. 72.

35. Kenneth Allott, "Matthew Arnold's 'Stagirius' and Saint-Marc Girardin," *Review of English Studies*, n.s. IX (August, 1958), 286-90.

36. The indispensable commentary on this poem is Arnold's own manuscript note quoted in *Commentary*, p. 25.

37. *Letters to Clough*, p. 59.

38. *Passages in a Wandering Life*, p. v.

39. *Life and Correspondence of John Duke Lord Coleridge*, I, 77.

40. "Arthur Hugh Clough: A Sketch," *Nineteenth Century*, XLIII (January, 1898), 106.

41. *Ibid.*, p. 107.

42. *Letters to Clough*, p. 93.

43. *Passages in a Wandering Life*, p. 57.

44. Mrs. Humphry Ward, *A Writer's Recollections* (2 vols. New York, 1918), I, 15.

45. *Unpublished Letters of Matthew Arnold*, ed. Arnold Whitridge (New Haven, Conn., 1923), pp. 65-66.

46. Ward, I, 70.

47. Woodward, *The Age of Reform*, p. 488.

48. Stanley, II, 9 (note).

49. Quoted in Kathleen Tillotson, "Rugby 1850: Arnold, Clough, Walrond, and In Memoriam," *Review of English Studies,* n.s. IV (April, 1953), 106-07.

50. Ward, I, 69.

51. *Letters to Clough,* p. 55.

52. *Ibid.,* pp. 56-57.

Chapter Two

1. Chambers, p. 9.

2. "George Sand," *Mixed Essays, Irish Essays, and Others* (New York, 1883), pp. 238-39.

3. *Letters,* I, 106.

4. *Letters,* II, 131.

5. "George Sand," p. 241.

6. *Ibid.,* p. 243.

7. *Ibid.,* p. 249.

8. "The French Play in London," *Mixed Essays, Irish Essays, and Others,* p. 432. See also *Commentary,* pp. 138-39.

9. "The French Play in London," pp. 434, 433.

10. *The Correspondence of Arthur Hugh Clough,* ed. Frederick L. Mulhauser (2 vols. Oxford, 1957), I, 178-79.

11. Patrick J. McCarthy, *Matthew Arnold and the Three Classes* (New York and London, 1964), gives a valuable account of Arnold and the Whig aristocracy.

12. Ward, I, 65-66.

13. *Letters to Clough,* p. 67.

14. "To a Republican Friend, 1848,—Continued," *The Poetical Works of Matthew Arnold,* ed. C. B. Tinker and H. F. Lowry (London and New York, 1950), p. 7. (Hereafter referred to as *Poetical Works.*)

15. *Letters,* I, 5.

16. *Letters,* I, 7.

17. *Commentary,* p. 33.

18. *Letters to Clough,* p. 69.

19. *Poetical Works,* p. 7.

20. *Letters,* I, 5, 6.

21. See Kenneth Allott, "Matthew Arnold's Reading Lists in Three Early Diaries," *Victorian Studies,* II (1959), 261 and note 23.

22. *Letters to Clough,* p. 69. Cf. "Resignation," lines 247-55, *Poetical Works,* p. 59.

23. Chambers, p. 38.

24. *Unpublished Letters,* pp. 16-17.

25. *Poetical Works,* p. 190.

26. *Letters to Clough*, p. 84.
27. *Letters to Clough*, p. 97.
28. *Letters*, I, 376.
29. *Poetical Works*, p. 42.
30. *Mixed Essays, Irish Essays, and Others*, p. 242.
31. Douglas Bush, *Mythology and the Romantic Tradition in English Poetry* (Cambridge, Mass., 1937), p. 249.
32. *Mixed Essays, Irish Essays, and Others*, p. 244.
33. *Commentary*, p. 89.
34. *Ibid.*, p. 162.
35. Leon Gottfried, *Matthew Arnold and the Romantics* (London, 1963), pp. 218-23.
36. H. V. Routh, *Towards the Twentieth Century: Essays in the Spiritual History of the Nineteenth* (New York and Cambridge, England, 1937), p. 194.

Chapter Three

1. March 6, 1849. Quoted in *Letters to Clough*, p. 127, note 3.
2. *Correspondence of Arthur Hugh Clough*, I, 246-47.
3. *Passages in a Wandering Life*, p. 63.
4. *Letters to Clough*, p. 129.
5. *Letters*, I, 5.
6. *Letters to Clough*, p. 95.
7. *Ibid.*
8. *Ibid.*, p. 111.
9. *Unpublished Letters*, p. 18.
10. E. M. Sellars, *Recollections and Impressions* (London, 1897), pp. 151-52. For Arnold's impressions of Charlotte Brontë, see his witty remarks in *Letters to Clough*, pp. 132-33.
11. *Letters to Clough*, p. 116.
12. *Ibid.*, p. 117.
13. *Correspondence of Arthur Hugh Clough*, I, 286.
14. *Commentary*, pp. 169-70.
15. *Correspondence of Arthur Hugh Clough*, I, 290.
16. *Letters*, I, 17.
17. Sellars, p. 152.
18. (Dolphin Books, New York [n.d.]), p. 9.
19. W. F. Connell, *The Educational Thought and Influence of Matthew Arnold* (London, 1950), p. 5.
20. Woodward, pp. 460-61.
21. *Letters to Clough*, p. 125.
22. *Reports on Elementary Schools*, ed. Sir Francis Sandford (London, 1889), p. 2.

23. *Essays, Letters, and Reviews by Matthew Arnold,* ed. Fraser Neiman (Cambridge, Mass., 1960), pp. 308-09.

24. *Ibid.,* p. 308.

25. William B. Guthrie, *Matthew Arnold's Diary, the Unpublished Items: a Transcription and Commentary* (4 vols. Unpublished Dissertation, University of Virginia, 1957), II, 369, 126, 127. (This dissertation is available on University of Michigan Microfilm.) See Sandford, *Reports,* pp. 29-30, 80.

26. *Letters,* I, 23.

27. Sandford, *Reports,* p. 233. See H. F. Lowry, Karl Young, and W. H. Dunn, *The Note-Books of Matthew Arnold* (London and New York, 1952), p. 350.

28. *Letters,* I, 103.

29. See Connell, p. 223.

30. *Ibid.,* pp. 255-56. For a general discussion see *The Complete Prose Works of Matthew Arnold,* ed. R. H. Super (Ann Arbor, Michigan, 1960-), IV, 344-48. Hereafter referred to as *Prose Works.*

31. *Unpublished Letters,* pp. 32-33.

32. *Letters,* I, 198.

33. Chambers, p. 21. *Letters,* I, 359, 360, 362; II, 9, 12-13.

34. *Letters,* I, 172.

35. *Letters,* I, 155.

36. Evidence of Arnold's esteem of *The Popular Education of France* is his sending a copy, together with *On Translating Homer,* to Sainte-Beuve in 1861. See Louis Bonnerot, *Matthew Arnold, Poète* (Paris, 1947), pp. 527-28.

37. William E. Buckler, *Matthew Arnold's Books: Towards a Publishing Diary* (Geneva, 1958), p. 68.

38. *Prose Works,* II, 24.

39. *Ibid.,* II, 29.

40. *Ibid.,* II, 263.

41. *Letters,* I, 231.

42. *Prose Works,* II, 320.

43. *Ibid.,* II, 325.

44. *Ibid.,* II, 319.

45. *Letters,* II, 152.

46. *Mixed Essays, Irish Essays, and Others,* p. 377.

47. Sandford, *Reports,* p. 259.

Chapter Four

1. *Letters,* II, 9.

2. *Letters to Clough,* p. 124.

3. *Unpublished Letters,* p. 18.

4. *Letters to Clough,* p. 88. This letter is correctly dated by A. Dwight Culler, *Imaginative Reason* (New Haven and London, 1966), p. 267, n. 17.

5. *Letters to Clough,* p. 99.

6. *Letters,* I, 179.

7. Clough made a valid comment about Wordsworth when he said: "These phenomena of external nature, which in the old and great poets come forward simply as analogies and similitudes of what is truly great, namely, human nature and as expressions of curious and wonderful relations, are in Wordsworth themselves the truly great, all-important, and pre-eminently wonderful things of the universe." Quoted in Katherine Chorley, *Arthur Hugh Clough; The Uncommitted Mind* (Oxford, 1962), p. 160.

8. *Letters,* I, 249.

9. The reader who wishes an interesting and sympathetic treatment of the Marguerite episode should read Iris Sell's *Matthew Arnold and France* or Isobel Macdonald's novel *The Buried Life;* but both should be tempered by the scholarship of Tinker and Lowry's *Commentary.*

10. *Letters,* II, 321.

11. *Letters to Clough,* p. 136.

12. See *Commentary,* pp. 106 ff.

13. *Commentary,* p. 287.

14. *Letters to Clough,* p. 111.

15. *Poetical Works,* p. xvii (*Prose Works,* I, 1).

16. *Commentary,* p. 291.

17. *Letters,* I, 30.

18. *Ibid.*

19. *Letters to Clough,* p. 140.

20. *Ibid.,* p. 144.

21. *Poetical Works,* p. xvii. (*Prose Works,* I, 1.)

22. *Matthew Arnold,* p. 318.

23. "Bishop Butler and the Zeit-Geist," *St. Paul & Protestantism . . . and Last Essays on Church & Religion* (New York, 1883), p. 276.

24. *Letters,* II, 142-43.

25. "Bishop Butler and the Zeit-Geist," pp. 275-76; *Note-Books,* p. 34.

26. *Poetical Works,* p. xix. (*Prose Works,* I, 3.)

27. *Poetical Works,* p. xix-xx. (*Prose Works,* I, 4.)

28. *Poetical Works,* p. xxiii. (*Prose Works,* I, 7.)

29. F. W. Bateson, *Poetry and the English Language* (Oxford, 1934), p. 105.

30. *Letters to Clough,* pp. 122-23.

31. *Ibid.,* p. 146.
32. "Preface to Merope," *Prose Works,* I, 59.
33. "On Translating Homer," *Prose Works,* I, 102.
34. *Letters to Clough,* p. 97. See H. W. Garrod, *Keats* (Oxford, 1926), pp. 95-97, and G. H. Ford, *Keats and the Victorians* (New Haven, Conn., 1944), pp. 81-83.

Chapter Five

1. *Letters to Clough,* pp. 120, 128, 138, 123.
2. *Unpublished Letters,* pp. 31-32.
3. *Letters,* I, 51.
4. Ward, I, 76. See Fraser Neiman, "'My Dear Sumner': Three Letters from Matthew Arnold," *Victorian Newsletter* (Spring 1960), pp. 28-30.
5. *Prose Works,* III, 290.
6. *Letters,* II, 135-36.
7. *Letters,* I, 331; London *Times,* 3 July 1862, p. 8. See *Essays, Letters, and Reviews by Matthew Arnold,* pp. 21-35, and *Prose Works,* III, 397-98.
8. See *Prose Works,* I, 225.
9. *Matthew Arnold's Books,* p. 154.
10. *Prose Works,* I, 25.
11. Ralph Barton Perry, *The Thought and Character of William James* (2 vols. Boston, 1935), I, 407.
12. *Prose Works,* I, 28.
13. *Ibid.,* I, 20.
14. *Ibid.*
15. See *Prose Works,* I, 225-26.
16. *Prose Works,* I, 34.
17. See *Commentary,* pp. 292-97, 340-47.
18. *Letters,* I, 57.
19. *Commentary,* pp. 277-85; *Prose Works,* I, 228-29.
20. *Letters,* I, 60.
21. *Letters,* I, 57. See Trilling's comment on the "fixity" of *Merope* (*Matthew Arnold,* p. 157).
22. Trilling, p. 164.
23. *Letters,* I, 126.
24. *Prose Works,* I, 97.
25. *Ibid.,* I, 136.
26. *Prose Works,* I, 188.
27. *Prose Works,* III, 234.
28. *Letters to Clough,* p. 115.

29. *Prose Works*, I, 103.
30. *Ibid.*, p. 215.
31. *Letters*, I, 126.
32. *Ibid.*, I, 139.
33. *Ibid.*, I, 199.
34. *Ibid.*, I, 172-73.
35. *Matthew Arnold's Books*, p. 67.
36. *Letters*, I, 247.
37. *Prose Works*, III, 258.
38. *Ibid.*, III, 283.
39. *North American Review*, CI (July, 1865), 212.
40. *Prose Works*, III, 108, 110.
41. *Ibid.*, III, 113.
42. W. H. G. Armytage, "Matthew and Richard Cobden in 1864: Some Recently Discovered Letters," *Review of English Studies*, XXV (July, 1949), 252.
43. *Ibid.*, p. 253.
44. *Prose Works*, III, 231.
45. *Ibid.*, III, 290.
46. *Ibid.*, III, 386.
47. *Ibid.*, III, 394.
48. *Ibid.*, III, 395.
49. *Letters*, I, 351.
50. Henry Adams, *The Education of Henry Adams* (New York, 1931), p. 358.

Chapter Six

1. *Letters*, II, 146.
2. See *Commentary*, p. 240.
3. *Letters*, I, 142.
4. *Ibid.*, I, 201.
5. *Ibid.*, I, 219-20.
6. *Ibid.*, I, 344.
7. *Matthew Arnold's Books*, p. 87.
8. *Letters*, I, 247.
9. *Ibid.*, I, 395.
10. *Matthew Arnold's Books*, p. 91.
11. *Letters*, II, 11.
12. *Ibid.*
13. *Prose Works*, V, 235.
14. *Five Uncollected Essays of Matthew Arnold*, ed. Kenneth Allott (Liverpool, 1953), p. 65.

15. *Letters,* I, 306.
16. *Prose Works,* V, 252.
17. *Prose Works,* III, 275.
18. Frederic Harrison, *The Choice of Books and Other Literary Pieces* (London, 1886), p. 109.
19. *Letters,* I, 372.
20. *Prose Works,* V, 93.
21. *Ibid.,* V, 111.
22. *Ibid.,* V, 117.
23. *Ibid.,* V, 122.
24. *Ibid.,* V, 143.
25. *Ibid.,* V, 161.
26. *Ibid.,* V, 168.
27. *Ibid.,* V, 175.
28. *Ibid.,* V, 193.
29. *Ibid.,* V, 339.
30. *Ibid.,* V, 70-71.
31. *Ibid.,* V, 328.

Chapter Seven

1. Basil Willey, *More Nineteenth Century Studies: A Group of Honest Doubters* (London, 1956), p. 137.
2. Quoted in *Note-Books,* p. 207.
3. William Robbins, *The Ethical Idealism of Matthew Arnold* (Toronto, 1959), p. 7.
4. (London, 1883), p. 8.
5. *Ibid.*
6. *Ibid.,* p. 66.
7. *Ibid.,* pp. 76-77.
8. *Ibid.,* p. 77.
9. (New York, 1902), p. 73.
10. *Ibid.,* p. 140.
11. *Ibid.,* pp. 181-82.
12. *Letters,* I, 249.
13. *Literature and Dogma,* p. 297.
14. *God & the Bible* (New York, 1883), p. 7.
15. *Ibid.,* p. 50.
16. *Ibid.,* p. 141.
17. W. H. Mallock, *The New Republic,* ed. J. Max Patrick (Gainesville, Florida, 1950), pp. 23-24.
18. *St. Paul and Protestantism,* pp. 130-31.

19. R. W. Emerson, *Complete Works,* Centenary edition, (12 vols. Boston and New York, 1903-1904), IV, 185-86.

20. "The Church of England" in *St. Paul & Protestantism . . . and Last Essays on Church & Religion,* p. 312.

21. G. K. Chesterton, *The Victorian Age in Literature* (New York and London, 1913), p. 75.

22. T. S. Eliot, *The Use of Poetry and the Use of Criticism* (Cambridge, Mass., 1933), p. 97.

23. *Towards the Twentieth Century,* p. 228.

24. *The Victorian Age in Literature,* p. 76.

25. *Last Essays on Church & Religion,* p. 179.

26. *Ibid.,* p. 213.

27. "The Divided Tradition in English Literature," *PMLA,* LXXIII (March, 1958), 73.

28. *Note-Books,* p. 67.

29. F. H. Bradley, *Ethical Studies* (London, 1876), p. 283.

30. Gaylord C. LeRoy, *Perplexed Prophets* (Philadelphia, 1953), p. 50.

31. Dr. Thomas Arnold, *Introductory Lectures on Modern History* (Oxford, 1842), p. 180.

32. *Letters,* I, 3-4.

33. *Letters to Clough,* p. 95.

34. *Works,* Centenary edition (London, 1896-1899), I, 69.

35. See John Holloway, *The Victorian Sage: Studies in Argument* (London, 1953), p. 204.

36. Letter to Dr. Arnold from Rome, Jan. 21, 1834, in Frances, Baroness Bunsen, *A Memoir of Baron Bunsen* (2 vols. London, 1868), I, 394; Francis W. Newman, rev. of *Literature and Dogma, Fraser's Magazine,* LXXXVIII (July, 1873), 127.

37. Lionel Trilling's remarks *passim* in his *Matthew Arnold* on the Arnolds and history are valuable. Dr. Arnold's concept of history is discussed in Duncan Forbes, *The Liberal Anglican Idea of History* (Cambridge, England, 1952), and in Richard K. Barksdale's unpublished dissertation (Harvard, 1951) "Thomas Arnold as Historian."

38. "Dr. Stanley's Lectures on the Jewish Church," *Prose Works,* III, 76-77.

39. *Ibid.,* III, 77.

40. *Ibid.*

41. *St. Paul & Protestantism,* p. 24.

42. "Les Sciences de la nature et les sciences historiques," *Revue des deux mondes,* XLVII, 2 période (15 octobre 1863), 762; "La Crise religieuse au dix-neuvième siècle," *Revue des deux mondes,* 2 période (15 fevrier 1863), 811.

43. *St. Paul & Protestantism*, pp. 121-22.
44. *Ibid.*, p. 131.
45. *Ibid.*, p. xii.
46. *Ibid.*, p. xxvii.
47. *Literature and Dogma*, pp. xii-xiii.
48. *Mixed Essays, Irish Essays, and Others*, p. 35.
49. *St. Paul & Protestantism . . . and Last Essays . . .* , p. 301.

Chapter Eight

1. *Five Uncollected Essays*, p. 65.
2. *Letters*, II, 212.
3. *Matthew Arnold's Books*, pp. 159-60.
4. *Mixed Essays, Irish Essays, and Others*, p. vii. In the Preface to *Poems* (1853) Arnold speaks of "the more serious kinds of poetry" as being "pragmatic poetry, to use an excellent expression of Polybius" (*Prose Works*, I, 7).
5. "Irish Catholicism and British Liberalism," *Mixed Essays, Irish Essays, and Others*, p. 99.
6. "A French Critic on Goethe," *Mixed Essays, Irish Essays, and Others*, p. 215.
7. *Mixed Essays, Irish Essays, and Others*, p. 51.
8. *Ibid.*, p. 50.
9. *Note-Books*, p. 334.
10. *Ibid.*, pp. 340, 341.
11. *Letters*, I, 137.
12. *Letters*, II, 190.
13. *The History of the Peloponnesian War, by Thucydides*, ed. Dr. Thomas Arnold (3 vols. Oxford, 1830-1835), I, 636.
14. "The Incompatibles (I)," *Mixed Essays, Irish Essays, and Others*, p. 286.
15. "A Liverpool Address," *Five Uncollected Essays*, p. 79.
16. *Letters*, II, 200.
17. *Civilization in the United States*, p. 71.
18. Roger L. Brooks, "A Matthew Arnold Letter to James Russell Lowell. The Reason for the American Lecture Tour," *American Literature*, XXXI (November, 1959), 336-38.
19. *Letters*, II, 213. John Morley was at the time editor of the *Pall Mall Gazette*, for which Arnold wrote a few drama reviews under the signature "An Old Playgoer."
Accounts of the lecture tour are given by E. P. Lawrence, "An Apostle's Progress: Matthew Arnold in America," *Philological Quarterly*, X (January, 1931), 62-79; Lionel Trilling, *Matthew Arnold*,

pp. 392-405; and John Henry Raleigh, *Matthew Arnold and American Culture* (Berkeley, California, 1957), pp. 56-76. The American tour was managed by Richard D'Oyly Carte, not by P. T. Barnum as Amy Lowell disparagingly says in her *John Keats* (II, 125).

20. *Letters*, II, 266, 229, 244, 247, 242.
21. *Letters*, II, 264.
22. Quoted in Lawrence, p. 66.
23. *Letters*, II, 254.
24. *Letters to Clough*, p. 66.
25. *Ibid.*, p. 126.
26. *Prose Works*, II, 160.
27. T. W. Higginson, "A Cosmopolitan Standard," in *The New World and the New Book* (Boston, 1892), pp. 45-46.
28. *Discourses in America* (London, 1902), pp. 15-16.
29. *Ibid.*, p. 41.
30. *Ibid.*, p. 66.
31. *Ibid.*, pp. 69-70.
32. *Letters*, II, 236.
33. *Discourses in America*, p. 82.
34. *Ibid.*, p. 107.
35. *Ibid.*, p. 121.
36. *Ibid.*, p. 111.
37. *Ibid.*, p. 135.
38. *Letters*, II, 345.

Chapter Nine

1. *Letters*, II, 351.
2. *Letters*, II, 151-52.
3. *Letters*, II, 217.
4. *Mixed Essays, Irish Essays, and Others*, p. 346.
5. *Ibid.*, p. 385.
6. *Ibid.*, p. 384.
7. "The Nadir of Liberalism," *Essays, Letters, and Reviews*, p. 279.
8. *Mixed Essays, Irish Essays, and Others*, p. 284; "The Zenith of Conservatism," *Essays, Letters, and Reviews*, p. 322.
9. John Morley, *Recollections* (2 vols. New York, 1917), I, 129.
10. *Letters*, II, 278.
11. *Letters*, II, 283.
12. *Matthew Arnold's Books*, pp. 75, 76.
13. *Letters*, II, 378.
14. *Essays in Criticism, Second Series*, p. 202.
15. Frederic Harrison, *Tennyson, Ruskin, Mill and Other Literary Estimates* (London, 1899), p. 128.

16. Eliot, *The Use of Poetry*, p. 111.

17. Allen Tate, *On the Limits of Poetry* (New York, 1948), p. 19.

18. *Essays in Criticism, Second Series*, pp. 1-2.

19. T. S. Eliot, *Selected Essays* (London, 1934), p. 248.

20. *Essays in Criticism, Second Series*, p. 3.

21. *Ibid.*, p. 5.

22. *Ibid.*, p. 40.

23. *The Importance of Scrutiny*, ed. Eric Bentley (New York, 1948), p. 90.

24. Walter Raleigh, ed., *Johnson on Shakespeare* (London, 1908), p. 11.

25. *Essays in Criticism, Second Series*, p. 119.

26. *Ibid.*, p. 144.

27. *Ibid.*, pp. 203-04.

28. *Ibid.*, p. 202.

29. *The Letters of Henry James*, selected and edited by Percy Lubbock (2 vols. London, 1920), I, 125-26.

30. E. B. Burgum, *Symposium*, II (1931), 86-87.

31. *Letters*, II, 130.

32. *Matthew Arnold* (1949), p. 5.

33. *Letters*, I, 385; I, 280; II, 188; I, 320.

Selected Bibliography

PRIMARY SOURCES

The standard editions of the poetry are *The Poetical Works of Matthew Arnold*, edited by C. B. Tinker and H. F. Lowry, New York: Oxford University Press, 1950, and *The Poems of Matthew Arnold*, edited by Kenneth Allott, New York: Barnes and Noble, 1965. Allott's edition is the more complete, and is fully annotated.

The standard edition of the prose is *The Complete Prose Works of Matthew Arnold*, ed. R. H. Super, Ann Arbor: University of Michigan Press, 1960—(in process). It supersedes *The Works of Matthew Arnold*, 15 vols., London: Macmillan, 1903-4. *Essays, Letters, and Reviews by Matthew Arnold*, ed. Fraser Neiman, Cambridge, Mass.: Harvard University Press, 1960, contains some material not yet assimilated in the volumes that have appeared of *The Complete Prose Works*.

The Note-Books of Matthew Arnold, ed. H. F. Lowry, Karl Young, and W. H. Dunn, London and New York: Oxford University Press, 1952, is of great value for the intellectual interests of Arnold.

There is no edition of Arnold's collected correspondence. However, the following books are important:

G. W. Russell, ed. *Letters of Matthew Arnold, 1848-1888*. 2 vols. London: Macmillan, 1895.

Arnold Whitridge, ed. *Unpublished Letters*. New Haven, Conn.: Yale University Press, 1923.

H. F. Lowry, ed. *The Letters of Matthew Arnold to Arthur Hugh Clough*. London and New York: Oxford University Press, 1932.

William E. Buckler, ed. *Matthew Arnold's Books: Towards a Publishing Diary*. Geneva: Librairie Droz, 1958.

Matthew Arnold's Letters; A Descriptive Checklist by A. K. Davis, Jr., is scheduled for publication by the University Press of Virginia.

SECONDARY SOURCES

Alexander, Edward. *Matthew Arnold and John Stuart Mill*. New York:

Columbia University Press, 1965. Contrasts main exponents of nineteenth-century humanism and liberalism.

Allott, Kenneth. *Matthew Arnold*. London: Longmans, Green, 1955. Excellent, brief, closely written introduction to Arnold.

Anderson, Warren D. *Matthew Arnold and The Classical Tradition.* Ann Arbor: University of Michigan, 1965. Valuable interpretive commentary on Arnold's poems and poetical development.

Baum, Paull Franklin. *Ten Studies in the Poetry of Matthew Arnold.* Durham, North Carolina: Duke University Press, 1958. Interpretive comments on several important poems.

Beach, Joseph Warren. *The Concept of Nature in Nineteenth-Century English Poetry*. New York: Macmillan, 1936. Classic work containing a chapter on Arnold.

Bonnerot, Louis. *Matthew Arnold, Poète: Essai de Biographie Psychologique*. Paris: Didier, 1947. Most detailed biographical study of Arnold and one of the most thoughtful examinations of his poems. A basic work, fully documented.

Brown, Edward Killoran. *Matthew Arnold: A Study in Conflict*. Chicago: University of Chicago Press, 1948. Study of the nature and strategy of Arnold's "disinterestedness."

Brownell, W. C. "Matthew Arnold." *Victorian Prose Masters.* New York: C. Scribner's Sons, 1901. Standard essay dealing illuminatingly with Arnold's ideas and prose style.

Burgum, Edwin B. "The Humanism of Matthew Arnold," *Symposium*, II (January, 1931), 85-112. A wide-ranging essay. Sees Arnold ultimately as instinctively sensitive to esthetic values in criticism, but blunted by an overriding Evangelicalism.

Bush, Douglas. *Mythology and the Romantic Tradition*. Cambridge, Mass.: Harvard University Press, 1937. Examines allusively Arnold's poetic use of classical mythology.

Chambers, E. K. *Matthew Arnold, A Study*. Oxford: Clarendon Press, 1947. Compendium of factual information, both biographical and bibliographical.

Connell, W. F. *The Educational Thought and Influence of Matthew Arnold*. London: Routledge, 1950. Important specialized study.

Coulling, Sidney M. B. "The Evolution of *Culture and Anarchy*," *Studies in Philology*, LX (October, 1963), 637-68. Excellent analysis of the place of this volume in Arnold's developing interests.

———. "Matthew Arnold's 1853 Preface: Its Origin and Aftermath," *Victorian Studies*, VII (March, 1964), 233-63. Valuable examination of Arnold's response to the critics of his 1853 Preface.

Culler, A. Dwight. *Imaginative Reason: The Poetry of Matthew Arnold.*

New Haven and London: Yale University Press, 1966. Indispensable critical study, highly schematic but illuminating.

De Laura, David J. "Arnold and Carlyle," *PMLA*, LXXIX (March, 1964), 104-29. Discriminating examination of a particularly important intellectual relationship.

Eliot, T. S. "Matthew Arnold" in *The Use of Poetry and the Use of Criticism*. Cambridge, Mass.: Harvard University Press, 1933. A brilliant essay, condescending in tone, but full of provocative statements.

————. "Arnold and Pater," in *Selected Essays*. London: Faber and Faber, 1932. Indicates Arnold's relationship to the early twentieth-century American humanists.

Fairchild, Hoxie Neale. "Arnold." *Religious Trends in English Poetry;* Vol. IV: *1830-1880: Christianity and Romanticism in the Victorian Era*. New York: Columbia University, 1957. Lively discussion from high Anglo-Catholic point of view. Ethical and religious attitudes expressed mainly in Arnold's poetry, which is interpreted quite literally as biographical testimony. Fairchild's style exhibits a Chestertonian love of antithesis and paradox.

Faverty, Frederic E. *Matthew Arnold, the Ethnologist*. Evanston, Illinois: Northwestern University Press, 1951. Important study of *On the Study of Celtic Literature*, and a fine example of careful reading.

Gates, Lewis E. "Matthew Arnold." *Three Studies in Literature*. New York: Macmillan, 1899. Valuable still as introduction to Arnold's prose.

Gottfried, Leon. *Matthew Arnold and the Romantics*. London: Routledge and Kegan Paul, 1963. An important study, more comprehensive than the title suggests.

Harding, F. W. J., *Matthew Arnold, the Critic, and France*. Geneva: Librairie Droz, 1964. The fullest study of Arnold's relations with French culture.

Holloway, John. *The Victorian Sage: Studies in Argument*. London: Macmillan, 1953. An excellent study of stylistic devices in the prose writings.

Houghton, Walter E. *The Victorian Frame of Mind, 1830-1870*. New Haven, Connecticut: Yale University Press, 1957. The remarks on Arnold *passim* usefully place him in the context of his age.

James, David Gwilym. *Matthew Arnold and the Decline of English Romanticism*. Oxford: Clarendon Press, 1961. These four penetrating but ultimately hostile lectures afford a stimulating introduction to Arnold's thought and work.

Johnson, E. D. H. *The Alien Vision of Victorian Poetry*. Princeton,

New Jersey: Princeton University Press, 1952. Has valuable interpretive chapter on Arnold's poetry.

Johnson, Wendell Stacy. *The Voices of Matthew Arnold: An Essay in Criticism.* New Haven: Yale University Press, 1961. A thoughtful critical study of Arnold's poetry.

Jump, J. D. *Matthew Arnold.* London and New York: Longmans, Green, 1955. Brief, useful book; more sympathetic to Arnold as critic than as poet, but more revealing with reference to Arnold the man.

Kermode, Frank. *Romantic Image.* New York: Macmillan, 1957. Contains interesting comments on Arnold's connection with symbolist poetry.

Krook, Dorothea. "Christian Humanism: Matthew Arnold's *Literature and Dogma.*" "Messianic Humanism." *Three Traditions of Moral Thought.* Cambridge: Cambridge University Press, 1939. Thoughtful, interpretive essays that analyze without polemics or apology Arnold's religious position.

Leavis, Frank Raymond. *The Common Pursuit.* London: Chatto and Windus, 1952. Contains *passim* provocative strictures. Praises Arnold for his intelligence, but patronizing toward his poetic achievement.

———. "Matthew Arnold." *The Importance of Scrutiny.* Ed. Eric Bentley. New York: G. W. Stewart, 1948. Important defense of Arnold as critic, particularly against the depreciation of T. S. Eliot.

McCarthy, Patrick J. *Matthew Arnold and the Three Classes.* New York and London: Columbia University Press, 1964. Fresh approach that places Arnold against the background of sociological interests and political figures of his times.

Madden, William A. *Matthew Arnold: A Study of the Poetic Temperament in Victorian England.* Bloomington: Indiana University Press, 1967. Valuable study.

———. "The Divided Tradition of English Criticism," *PMLA,* LXXIII (March, 1958), 69-80. Interesting study of Arnold's position in the literary tradition of Pater and Yeats on the one hand; of Hulme and Eliot on the other.

Miller, J. Hillis. *The Disappearance of God: Five Nineteenth-Century Writers.* Cambridge, Mass.: Harvard University Press, 1963. Fresh, provocative approach.

Muir, Kenneth "Arnold and the Victorian Dilemma." *The Penguin New Writing.* Ed. John Lehman. London: Penguin Books, 1947. Sympathetic introduction to Arnold's poetry.

Mulhauser, Frederick L., ed. *The Correspondence of Arthur Hugh*

Clough. Oxford: Clarendon Press, 1957. Valuable source for personalities and currents of ideas in Clough's and Arnold's world.

Paul, Herbert W. *Matthew Arnold.* London: Macmillan and Co., 1902. Convenient, concise introduction to Arnold; objective in temper; but limited by early date of publication.

Perkins, David. "Arnold and the Function of Literature," *Journal of English Literary History,* XVIII (December, 1951), 267-309. Argues that Arnold "tried—to a degree unequalled by any other writer of the nineteenth century—to reassert both the ultimate end of human culture and also the indispensable place of the humanities, especially literature, as the means of attaining their end" (309).

Raleigh, John Henry. *Matthew Arnold and American Culture.* Berkeley and Los Angeles: University of California Press, 1957. Examines the response to Arnold of major American critics from Henry James, Jr., to Lionel Trilling.

Robbins, William. *The Ethical Idealism of Matthew Arnold: A Study of the Nature and Sources of His Moral Ideas.* Toronto: University of Toronto, 1959. Important study that takes seriously the religious writings of Arnold.

Saintsbury, George. *Matthew Arnold.* Edinburgh and London: William Blackwood and Sons, 1899. Brief, lucid, cavalier, and opinionated.

Sells, Iris Esther. *Matthew Arnold and France: The Poet.* Cambridge, England: University Press, 1935. A sympathetic and rather subjective book emphasizing the influence especially of George Sand and Senancour, on Arnold and romanticizing the Marguerite episode.

Stange, G. Robert. *Matthew Arnold: The Poet as Humanist.* Princeton: Princeton University Press, 1967. Comprehending, sympathetic study of Arnold's concepts of poetry, nature, self, and love.

Tate, Allen. *On the Limits of Poetry: Selected Essays, 1928-1948.* New York: Swallow Press, 1948. Comments *passim* on Arnold indicate some of Arnold's limitations as a technical critic.

Tillotson, Geoffrey. *Criticism and the Nineteenth Century.* London: Athlone Press, 1951. Extensive comments on Arnold's poetry and prose.

Tinker, C. B. and H. F. Lowry. *The Poetry of Matthew Arnold: A Commentary.* London, New York, and Toronto: Oxford University Press, 1950. Invaluable for sources and genesis of the individual poems.

Trilling, Lionel. *Matthew Arnold.* New York: Columbia University Press, 1949. The standard basic critical work.

Warren, Alba H., Jr. *English Poetic Theory, 1825-1865.* Princeton: Princeton University Press, 1950. Discusses in illuminating detail the Preface to Arnold's *Poems* (1853).

Willey, Basil. *Nineteenth Century Studies.* London: Chatto and Windus, 1949. Chapter on Arnold's prose works.

Index

Abrams, Meyer H., 137
Alaric at Rome, 20-21
Alice, Princess, 105
Allott, Kenneth, 25
Amiel, Henri Frédéric, 153, 154
"Anarchy and Authority," 105
Aristotle, 76, 158
Arnold, Frances, 16, 21
Arnold, Frances Lucy Wightman, 49,
  51, 69, 142, 148, 154
Arnold, Jane Martha, 16, 21, 22, 44
Arnold, Lucy, 142, 148, 153
Arnold, Mary, 16
Arnold, Matthew, for events in life,
  See Chronology; poetry, *See* name
  of poem; prose, *See* name of prose
  work
Arnold, Richard Penrose, 142, 154
Arnold, Susanna, 16
Arnold, Thomas, 16-17, 21, 26-27,
  34, 47
Arnold, Dr. Thomas, 14, 15, 16, 20,
  22, 26, 27, 28, 48, 77, 92, 102, 125
Arnold, William Delafield, 17, 81
Athenaeum (London club), 81-82
Auden, W. H., 20
Aurelius Antoninus, Marcus, 148
"Austerity of Poetry, The," 101

"Bacchanalia," 104
"Balder Dead," 79
Balliol College, Oxford, 20, 21-28
"Barbarians, Philistines, Populace,"
  108
Barnum, P. T., 143
Bateson, F. W., 76

Bauer, Ferdinand Christian, 128
Béranger, Pierre-Jean de, 22, 27, 48
Bhagavad Gita, 34, 38, 48, 75
Bible, The, 75, 162
"Bishop Butler and the Zeit-Geist,"
  134
Bode, the Rev. John Ernest, 82
Bradley, Francis H., 117, 120
British Quarterly Review, 95
Brontë, Charlotte, 48
Brooks, Cleanth, 161
Brooks, Phillips, 143
Browning, Robert, 37, 58, 59, 100
Buckland, the Rev. John, 16
Buller, Sir John Yarde, 82
Bunsen, C. K. J., Baron von, 125
Burgum, E. B., 162
"Buried Life, The," 68-69
Burke, Edmund, 121, 125, 140, 152
Burns, Robert, 158
Bush, Douglas, 39
Butler, Arthur Gray, 28-29
Butler, Joseph, Bishop of Durham,
  56-57, 129, 134, 145; *See also*
  "Bishop Butler . . ."
Byron, George Gordon, Lord, 27, 65-
  66, 76, 139, 140, 154, 155, 158,
  159, 160, 161

"Cadmus and Harmonia," 59
Carlyle, Thomas, 15, 34, 48, 122-
  124, 125, 148
Carnegie, Andrew, 142, 143
"Caution to Poets, A," 104
Century Magazine, 153
Chartists, 34

Chaucer, Geoffrey, 85, 158
Chesterton, G. K., 118, 119
Child, Francis J., 143
Chopin, Frédéric, 30-31
"Civilisation in the United States," 149
Civilization in the United States: First and Last Impressions of America, 149
Clifford, the Honorable Charles, 110
Clanricarde, Marquis of, 110
Clough, Arthur Hugh, 19, 22, 26, 31, 33, 34, 46, 59, 71, 102; letters to, 29, 32-34, 36, 37, 47-48, 50-51, 60, 62, 65, 74, 84, 91, 121, 122, 123, 144
Cobden, Richard, 97
Coleridge, John Duke, 23-24, 26, 154
Coleridge, Samuel Taylor, 16, 160
Colvin, Sidney, 139
Condorcet, Jean A. N., Marquis de, 136-137
Cornhill Magazine, 98, 100, 105, 110
Cowley, Lord, 89
Craik, George L., 153
Creweian orations, 83
Culture and Anarchy, 54, 85, 94, 104-109, 111, 138, 142, 151
"Culture and Its Enemies," 100, 107
Curtis, George, 162

Dante, Alighieri, 90-91, 158
Decade (debating society), 26
"Democracy," 53-54
Denison, George Anthony, Archdeacon, 82
DeQuincey, Thomas, 16
Derby, Lord, *See* Stanley, Edward, Lord
Deutsch, E. M. O., 104
Devonshire, 23
Dickens, Charles, 16
Discourses in America, 145-148
"Disestablishment in Wales," 153
Disraeli, Benjamin, 105
Dixon, Hepworth, 110

"Dr. Stanley's Lectures on the Jewish Church," 124, 126, 128, 130
"Doing as One Likes," 108
"Dover Beach," 43, 59, 64, 68, 100, 101, 156
Dowden, Edward, 154
Dryden, John, 104, 158
Durrell, Lawrence, 45

"Ecce Convertimur ad Gentes," 56
Edinburgh Review, 95
Elcho, Lord, 110
Eliot, George, 15
Eliot, T. S., 118-119, 155, 156, 161
Emerson, Ralph Waldo, 27, 34, 144, 145
"Emerson," 145, 147-148
"Empedocles on Etna," 58-59, 62, 71-75, 79, 85, 100, 103, 104, 107
Empedocles on Etna, and Other Poems, 60, 61-74
Encyclopedia Britannica, 153
England and the Italian Question, 89, 121
Epictetus, 34, 37, 45
"Equality," 138
Essays in Criticism (1865), 82-83, 93-98, 103
Essays in Criticism, Second Series, 153-161

"Faded Leaves," 69-70
Faucit, Helena, 86
Fitzgerald, Edward, 59
Fletcher, Mary, 20
Fontanès, Ernest, 101
"Forsaken Merman, The," 43, 59, 71
Forster, William E., 16, 93
Forster, Mrs. William E., *See* Arnold, Jane
Fortnightly Review, 30-31, 106-107, 138, 151, 153
"Fragment of an 'Antigone,'" 39, 41, 42
Fraser's Magazine, 65, 100

Index

"French Critic on Goethe, A," 137

"French Critic on Milton, A," 137

French Eton, A, 53, 54-56, 94, 103, 121, 124, 128, 144

Friendship's Garland, 104, 106, 109-112

"From Easter to August," 152

Froude, Hurrell, 46

Froude, James Anthony, 46

"Function of Criticism at the Present Time, The," 85, 94-95, 96, 104, 147, 155, 157

"Future, The," 121, 124

"General Report for the Year 1882," 56-57

"George Sand," 137

Gladstone, William Ewart, 52, 152, 163

Glanville, Joseph, 78

God and the Bible, 114, 116-117, 133

Goethe, Johann Wolfgang von, 16, 27, 34, 35, 63, 65-66, 68, 76, 77, 96, 98, 120, 121, 126, 127, 128, 130, 148, 162

Grant, Gen. Ulysses S., 142, 153

Granville, Lord, *See* Leveson-Gower, Granville George

Gray, Thomas, 154, 158

Grimm, Hermann, 138

"Guide to English Literature, A," 137

Guizot, François P. G., 89

Harrison, Frederic, 56, 106-107, 110, 155

Hawker, J. Manley, 23

Hawkins, Dr. Edward, 18

Hay, John, 143

"Hebraism and Hellenism," 109

Hegel, Georg W. F., 121, 126, 127

Heine, Heinrich, 35, 161

"Heinrich Heine," 96

Herder, Johann Gottfried von, 121

Hesiod, 75

Higginson, Thomas Wentworth, 142, 144-145, 155

Hill, Herbert, 20

Holmes, Oliver Wendell, 142, 143

Homer, 34, 37, 45, 77, 89-91, 120

Hooker, Richard, 129, 132

Hopkins, Gerard Manley, 102

Horace, 85

Howells, William Dean, 144

Hugo, Victor, 138

Humboldt, Wilhelm von, 108

Hume, David, 121

Hunt, G. W., 139

Huxley, Thomas Henry, 146-147

"In Harmony with Nature," 38

"In Utrumque Paratus," 38, 123

Ipswich Working Men's College, 56

Irish Essays and Others, 137, 151

James, Henry, Jr., 13, 14, 96, 141, 142, 144, 161

James, William, 84

Johnson, Samuel, 145, 159

Jowett, Benjamin, 26, 119

Kay, James, 50

Keats, John, 60, 76, 78-79, 139, 154, 159, 160

Keble, the Rev. John, 14, 18, 27-28, 82

Kingsmill, Hugh (pseud. of Lunn, Hugh Kingsmill), 87-88

Lacordaire, Jean Baptiste Henri de, 89

Lake, William Charles, 24, 26

Lamb, Charles, 16

Lansdowne, Lord, *See* Petty-Fitzmaurice, Henry

Last Essays on Church and Religion, 114, 134, 137

Laveleye, Émile de, 129

Leavis, F. R., 159, 161

Leighton, Frederick, 139
Letters, Speeches, and Tracts on Irish Affairs by Edmund Burke, 140
Leveson-Gower, Granville George, Lord Granville, 52
"Lines Written in Kensington Gardens," 66-67
"Lines Written on the Seashore at Eaglehurst," 21
Lingen, Robert R. W., 52
"Literary Influence of Academies, The," 91, 96
Literature and Dogma, 114, 115-116, 120, 124, 128, 131, 133
"Literature and Science," 145, 146-147
Locke, John, 48-49
Lowe, Robert, Viscount Sherbrooke, 52, 110
Lowell, James Russell, 142, 144
Lucas, the Rev. William, 82
Lucretius, 34, 85, 86
Luther, Martin, 141
Lyell, Sir Charles, 15

Macaulay, Thomas Babington, 15, 16, 138
Macmillan, Alexander, 53
Macmillan and Company, 153
Macmillan's Magazine, 54, 100, 153
Madden, William A., 119
Maistre, Joseph Marie, Comte de, 151
Mallock, William H., 56, 117
Marx, Karl, 121, 133
Melville, Herman, 144
"Memorial Verses," 62, 64-66
Merope, 60, 77, 86-88
Miall, Edward, 110
Michelet, Jules, 121, 144
Mill, John Stuart, 50
Milman, Henry Hart, 15
Milton, John, 138, 153, 154, 157, 158
Mixed Essays, 137, 151
"Modern Sappho, A," 42
"Morality," 66

Morley, John, 30, 152
Müller, Friedrich Max, 22
"My Countrymen," 110
"Mycerinus," 39-40

"Nadir of Liberalism, The," 152
"Natalis dies Bonzensis," 21
National Review, 153
New Poems, 100-104
Newcastle Commission, 52, 89
Newman, Francis W., 89-90, 91-92
Newman, John Henry, 15, 22, 27-28, 125, 129-130, 148
Nicolson, Sir Harold, 61
Niebuhr, Barthold Georg, 76, 121, 125
Nineteenth Century, 141, 148, 149, 151, 152, 153
North American Review, 96
Norton, Charles Eliot, 143, 153, 161-162
Note-Books, 119, 121, 133, 139, 162
"Numbers," 142, 145-146

"Obermann Once More," 102, 103
"On the Modern Element in Literature," 83-86
On the Study of Celtic Literature, 83, 98-99
On Translating Homer, 83, 89-91, 94
On Translating Homer: Last Words, 83, 89, 91
Oriel College, Oxford, 24, 31-32
Oxford University, 82-86, 89-91, 98, 100; *See also* Balliol College, Oriel College
"Our Liberal Practitioners," 109

Pall Mall Gazette, 106, 109-110
"Palladium," 100, 101-102
Parmenides, 126
Pater, Walter, 95, 139, 156
Petty-Fitzmaurice, Henry, Lord Lansdowne, 32-35, 50
"Philomela," 74, 78
"Pis-Aller," 104
Plato, 147

Index

Poems (1853), 60, 69, 74-79, 84, 85; Preface, 154, 155
Poems. Second Series (1855), 60, 69, 79
Poetry of Arnold, *See* titles of poems and of collections
Pope, Alexander, 104, 158
Popular Education of France, The, 53, 144
"Porro Unum est Necessarium," 108
"Progress," 124-125
Prose Works of Arnold, *See* titles of essays and collections
"Psychological Parallel, A," 134
"Puritanism and the Church of England," 129

Quarterly Review, 95, 116
"Quiet Work," 38, 66
Quillinan, Edward, 64

Rachel, Elisa Félix, 31
"Rachel," 100
Ralegh, Sir Walter, 84
Raleigh, John Henry, 144
Reform Bill of 1832, 15
"Religious Isolation," 43
Renan, Ernest, 15, 30, 89, 121, 128, 145
Reports on Elementary Schools, 1852-1882, 53
"Requiescat," 74, 78
"Resignation," 31, 34, 43-45, 64
Reuss, Édouard, 128
"Revolutions," 61, 124
Revue des Deux Mondes, 95
Richards, I. A., 161
Rintoul, R. S., 75
Robbins, William, 114-115
Robinson, Henry Crabb, 99
Rothschild, Louisa, Lady de, 93, 94, 105
Routh, H. V., 45, 119, 161
"Rude Orator," 25
"Rugby Chapel," 102, 104

Rugby School, 17-20, 28-29, 81
Ruskin, John, 81, 157
Russell, John, Lord, 32, 50, 74

St. Paul and Protestantism, 112, 114-115, 117-118, 124, 128, 130-132
Sainte-Beuve, Charles Augustin, 27, 62, 89, 153
Sand, George, 22, 25-26, 27, 30-31, 39, 45, 62, 75; *See also* "George Sand"
Sandford, Sir Francis, 53
Saturday Review, 92
Scherer, Edmond, 137, 138
Schiller, J. C. Friedrich von, 75
"Scholar-Gipsy, The," 59, 71, 74, 77, 78-79, 82, 85, 100
Schools and Universities on the Continent, 53, 121
Scott, Sir Walter, 16
"Second-Best, The," 68
"Self-Deception," 61
"Self-Dependence," 66, 68
Senancour, Étienne Pivert de, 34, 47, 48, 62, 102, 148
Sewell, William, 46
Shairp, John Campbell, 26, 71-72
Shakespeare, William, 37, 76, 157, 158
"Shakespeare," 25
Shelley, Percy Bysshe, 60, 153, 154, 155, 159, 160
"Sick King in Bokhara, The," 39-41
Six Chief Lives from Johnson's "Lives of the Poets," The, 140
Smith, Elder and Company, 112
Smith, George, 105, 110, 137
Smith, Goldwin, 99, 110
"Sohrab and Rustum," 42, 59, 74, 77-78, 79
Sophocles, 34, 37, 45, 84, 86
Spectator, The, 75, 116
Spinoza, Benedict (Baruch) de, 49, 126, 127, 149
Staël, Madame de, 89

"Stagyrus," 25
Stanley, Arthur P., Dean, 18, 19, 26, 79, 100; *See also* "Dr. Stanley's Lectures . . ."
Stanley, Edward, Lord (Earl of Derby), 110, 140
"Stanzas from the Grande Chartreuse," 59, 100, 101
"Stanzas in Memory of the Author of 'Obermann,' " 62-65, 67
Stedman, Edmund Clarence, 144
Stephen, Fitzjames, 102
Strauss, David Friedrich, 15, 128
"Strayed Reveller, The," 31, 35-37
Strayed Reveller, and Other Poems, The, 35-45, 68, 100
"Study of Poetry, The," 85, 90, 139, 140, 148, 155-159
"Summer Night, A," 66, 67-68, 136
Sumner, the Rev. George Henry, 82
"Sweetness and Light," 107-108
Swinburne, Algernon C., 14
"Switzerland," 43, 47, 69-70

Tate, Allen, 155, 161
Tauler, Johann, 153
Temple, Frederick, 26
Tennyson, Alfred, Lord, 16, 35, 58, 59, 60
Thackeray, William Makepeace, 105
Thomas à Kempis, 133, 162
Thucydides, 84, 121
"Thyrsis," 59, 82, 100, 102-103, 121
Times, London, 55, 152
Tinker, C. B. and H. F. Lowry, 21, 25, 41, 69, 72, 78
"To a Friend," 31
"To a Gipsy Child by the Sea-Shore," 38
"To a Republican Friend," 34
"To Marguerite, . . ." 47, 69
Tolstoi, Leo, 153, 154-155
Trilling, Lionel, 75, 89, 114, 145, 150, 153, 163
"Tristram and Iseult," 43, 62, 70-71
Twain, Mark, 144

"Up to Easter," 152

Vergil, 76, 85
Voltaire, François Marie Arouet de, 141

Walford, Edward, 21-22
Walrond, Theodore, 26
Ward, Mrs. Humphry, 17, 154
Ward, T. H., 140, 154, 155
Ward, W. W., 118
"Westminster Abbey," 100
Westminster Review, 92-93, 116
Whitman, Walt, 144
Whitridge, Frederick W., 148
Whittier, John Greenleaf, 143
Wightman, Frances Lucy, *See* Arnold, Frances Lucy Wightman.
Wightman, Sir William, 49, 52-53, 92, 93
Wilberforce, William, 15
Willey, Basil, 114
Wilson, Thomas, Bishop, 162
Wimsatt, W. K., 161
"Wish, A," 104
Wolf, Friedrich, 90
"Word about America, A," 141-142, 144, 148
"Word More about America, A," 148, 149
Wordsworth, William, 16, 18, 27, 35, 43, 63, 65-66, 67, 75-76, 139, 140, 154, 158, 159-160, 162
"World and the Quietist, The," 38
Wright, Ichabod C., 90
"Written in Butler's Sermons," 43, 68
"Written in Emerson's Essays," 43

"Youth of Man, The," 66
"Youth of Nature, The," 66

"Zenith of Conservatism, The," 152
Zincke, the Rev. F. Barham, 56